First Children

First Children

GROWING UP IN THE WHITE HOUSE

by Katherine Leiner

PORTRAITS BY KATIE KELLER

TAMBOURINE BOOKS
NEW YORK

To my children, Dylan and Makenna,
both of them firsts

LIBRARY OF CONGRESS CATALOGING IN PUBLICATION DATA
Leiner, Katherine.
First children / by Katherine Leiner; illustrations by Katie Keller. — 1st ed.   p. cm.
Summary: Anecdotes from the lives of children who have lived in the
White House from the time of George Washington to the present.
1. Children of presidents—United States—Biography—Juvenile literature.
[1. Children of presidents.] I. Keller, Katie, ill. II. Title.
E176.45.L45 1996 973'.099—dc20 [b] 95-30652 CIP AC
ISBN 0-688-13341-X

1 3 5 7 9 10 8 6 4 2
First edition

Author's Note

In the eighteenth, nineteenth, and early twentieth centuries, Americans described each other differently than they do today. In order to maintain authenticity, I have used such words as "Indian," "squaw," "Colored," or "black" to describe Native Americans and African-Americans when the material calls for these descriptions. Although these are sometimes considered offensive terms now, they were in common use in those times.

Acknowledgments

I am grateful to the following people for their careful reading and their time. Their patience with the work was remarkable.

Special thanks to my very fine and diligent editor, Paulette Kaufmann; my dear friend Liza Ketchum; my son, Dylan Leiner, who acted as research assistant; and my daughter, Makenna, who always makes me laugh and cry when I need it.

I am also extremely grateful to all of the following people and the institutes and organizations with which they work:

Paul Arbor, *Life* Magazine Photos; Cyndy Bittinger at the Calvin Coolidge Memorial Foundation, Inc.; Don Bowden at AP/Wide World Photos; Jim Cedrone at the John F. Kennedy Library; Elaine Clark, National Park Service: Andrew Johnson National Historical Site; Ruth Corcoran, the White House Historical Association; Mary Beth Corrigan, Historical Library of Washington D.C.; Culver Research Service; Wallace Dailey, Theodore Roosevelt Collection—The Houghton Library, Harvard University; Allen Fisher, Lyndon B. Johnson Library; Eileen Flanagan, Chicago Historical Society; Julie Gates; Gil Gonzales, Rutherford B. Hayes Presidential Center; Debbie Goodsite, Bettman Archives; Ray Henderson, National Park Service; Jerry at The Film Box; Christine Meadows, Curator of Mount Vernon Ladies Association of the Union; Elizabeth Mixon; Carolyn Parsons, Picture Collections, Virginia State Library and Archives; Karen V. E. Peters, Mount Vernon Ladies Association of the Union; Lucia Poole; Holly Reed, National Archives; Mark Renovitch, Franklin D. Roosevelt Library; Rex Scouten, White House Curator; Dr. William Seale; Anne Sindelar, Western Reserve Historical Society; Daniel J. Stanhope, Lyndon B. Johnson Library Archivist; Lucia Stanton, historian, Pat Nicholas, Suzanne Olson, Zanne Macdonald, Anne Lucas, and Tracy Via at Thomas Jefferson Memorial Foundation; Chris Steele, Massachussetts Historical Society; Stock Montage; Kathleen Struss, Dwight D. Eisenhower Library; Carolyn Texely, Louis A. Warren Lincoln Library; Kay Tyler, Sherwood Forest Plantation; and Vernon Will, Ohio Historical Society Archives.

Introduction

The White House around 1827

The White House is the most famous home in the United States of America. All of our Presidents have lived in it except for George Washington, who selected the area for the Federal City and initiated the architectural plans for the White House.

The White House has 132 rooms and over 100 household employees, including clerks, accountants, managers, butlers, housemaids, cooks, plumbers, and gardeners. The facilities available for the President and his family's use in the huge house include a barbershop, a beauty salon, an outdoor swimming pool, an exercise gym, a bowling alley in the basement, a 45-seat movie theater, a putting green on the South Lawn, a tennis court, a horseshoe court, and a new jogging track. A completely staffed medical clinic is available 24 hours a day.

Important foreign dignitaries visit the First Family, along with over one million tourists who walk through the historic rooms on the first floor every year. Night after night there are concerts and parties and continuous celebrations that call for the presence of the President, the First Lady, and, oftentimes, the "First Children." Many personal friends come to stay the night in the private quarters on the second floor.

What is it like to grow up in the midst of all of this? What is it really like to be a child in the White House? What is it like to grow up with the world watching?

Almost 190 children, from infants to young adults, have spent at least part of their childhoods in the White House. They have been Presidents' children and grandchildren, nieces and nephews, and, occasionally, children of close friends or Presidential staff. Living in the White House seems to magnify the experiences of childhood. Many First Children have complained that it is like living in a fishbowl where everyone watches your every move and then talks about you in the newspapers and at private parties as if they knew you.

President Ford's daughter, Susan, who was seventeen when she began living in the White House, said, "At times it seemed like a cross between a reform school and a convent."

Barbara Anne Eisenhower, President Eisenhower's granddaughter, said she felt that the South Lawn was her own private playground. One day, however, when a tour of people passed her as she zoomed along on her tricycle, they stopped and whispered and pointed. It made Barbara Anne feel uncomfortable, as if she were somehow on show for these strangers.

The White House, or Executive Mansion as it was called during the early years, is not only a home for the President, the First Lady, and their children, but is also an office. In some ways this makes the First Children's parents more readily available to them. If there is an emergency during the school day, their parents are usually close by. On the other hand, with their offices so near their home, as parents the President and First Lady can also be more preoccupied and unavailable even though they are close by.

It has been said that the Presidents and First Ladies who have lived with their children while they were in the White House were the happiest. But what about the children? Certainly, children who have lived in the White House are forever set apart in some ways from their peers. Whether it adds to their lives or makes life more difficult is hard to know. Some First Children, as they grew older, said it was the happiest time in their lives, while others hated living there. There have been First Children who have been ill, and some have even died while living in the the White House.

One thing is sure, children who lived in the White House before television did not have to contend with the media to the same extent as those who have lived there during the past forty years. Perhaps that gave the earlier First Children more privacy and helped them have more normal childhoods.

Of the forty-one Presidential families, I have chosen to write about seventeen. Most had children between the ages of four and sixteen, though I have also included chapters on Letitia Tyler, who was twenty-three, Luci Baines Johnson, who was nineteen, Lillian Rogers, who was the daughter of President Taft's upstairs maid, and several Presidential grandchildren. I didn't write about some families because, unhappily, there was very little material available. I have also chosen certain events during each of their stays that should allow readers to get a broader sense of what the United States and the world were like during that particular Presidential term.

Historians tend to agree that is it very hard to grow up in the White House. The White House children are treated as if they were bigger than life. And, in a way, those long hallways and winding staircases, the hidden nooks and crannies, the multitude of staff members, and the private jets and helicopters provide the fabric for a lifestyle that few other children in America will ever have. Yet these same things also provide a kind of magic spectacle for all of us as we catch a glimpse here and there of what it is like to live in the White House.

Table of Contents

First Children

A Plague in Philadelphia

*I*n August of 1793, a landowner living an ordinary life suddenly turned yellow and died on Philadelphia's waterfront. This was the beginning of the "yellow fever" epidemic.

Although the newspapers were full of yellow fever reports, fourteen-year-old Nellie Custis and her twelve-year-old brother, George "Little Wash" Custis, were protected from that news. They lived with their grandparents, George and Martha Washington, in the heart of downtown Philadelphia.

The Executive Mansion at 190 High Street was the Washingtons' third Presidential mansion since Nellie's grandfather came to office. It was originally built as a private home. It was large, but not large enough for the divided life of a President. The third floor was crowded with Nellie's grandfather's secretaries, and the hallways were always full of Presidential officials and dignitaries from all over the nation and sometimes the world. On the second floor where the President's family lived, Nellie often heard strange accents and pounding footsteps as visitors passed the private chambers at all hours of the night and day.

The Mansion was wedged tightly between another large private home and a hairdressing salon. Nellie tried to concentrate on her harpsichord, but the endless parade of colorful carriages outside her window constantly stole her

George Washington,
Martha Washington,
Nellie, and
"Little Wash" on the
porch of their
Philadelphia home

attention. The carriages paused at the salon to leave finely dressed ladies in brilliant long dresses and gentlemen in brocaded, knee-high breeches and cutaway coats; most of them had powdered faces and high, white-powdered wigs.

Nellie's day was split between practice on her harpsichord and the studies dealt out to her by her tutor, Tobias Lear. Otherwise, she and her dear friend Polly would have stood at Nellie's window, admiring the elegance and glamour of those who came and went from the hair salon all day. Polly, who was Mrs. Mary Lear, Tobias's wife, had come to live at the Mansion three years before when Tobias became one of the President's secretaries. She was a tremendous help to Nellie's grandmother with the daily chores and the rearing of both Nellie and Little Wash. And although she was six years older than Nellie, Polly's warm and playful presence endeared her to Nellie and they became fast friends. In March of 1791, Polly had given birth to a son, Benjamin Lincoln Lear, and Nellie helped Polly during those first few difficult days of new motherhood. The third floor, where Polly, Tobias, and the baby lived, was a noisy and busy place indeed.

While the rest of the Mansion was involved in work of one kind or another,

Little Wash frequently stole away from his studies to spy on his grandfather's meetings. Nellie often caught him hiding behind the long, heavy draperies or behind the open door, as quiet as the mice that scurried across his feet. However, Little Wash didn't stay hidden long. Rather than risk their grandfather's stern looks and booming voice if he were caught, he would rush off to the stables to visit the hands and help groom the horses.

Nellie's favorite times were when her two older sisters, Betsey and Martha, came to visit. Nellie's father had died suddenly in 1781 of high fever that he had contracted acting as an aid to his stepfather during the Revolutionary War. Grandmama and Grandpapa Washington had unoffically adopted her and Little Wash. Although Nellie knew it helped her widowed mother enormously to have her and her brother live with their grandparents, sometimes Nellie missed being with her sisters. When Betsey and Martha visited, the three sisters were inseparable. Polly joined them when she could get away from her baby for a few moments.

In the elegant old Mansion, Nellie watched her grandfather as he governed the new nation. During the days, with the curtains pulled open wide, and during the nights under brightly burning candled chandeliers, her grandfather and his staff often had their hands full. With all of the the government's most powerful people coming and going on a day-to-day basis, Nellie and Little Wash felt safe and protected.

Until yellow fever hit close to their home.

August 1793 was hot; hotter than it had been for many summers. And the high-necked clothes and fashionable powdered wigs didn't help. Everyone was looking for a cool spot of shade; even a puddle of water which was not mosquito infested would have been a welcome relief.

The disease had already spread among sailors, grog sellers, and the poor, and was beginning to reach out into other parts of the city, before doctors informed everyone of the yellow fever epidemic. Although Nellie's grandfather had been warned by his doctors, he would not allow himself to be caught up in the hysteria that was taking hold of the city, so life at 190 High Street continued as usual.

On August 10 Polly Lear came down with the fever. Nellie begged Grandmama to let her visit Polly's room, but her grandmother forbade her. There was nothing Nellie could do but wait. Polly's fever burned for days while Nellie agonized. When Polly died, Nellie wrote in her diary, "I cannot even write about it."

Nellie's grandfather still held firmly that the epidemic was not a serious threat to either his family or the citizens of the city. After many more of Washington's staff had taken ill, he conceded somewhat when he wrote, "*We are well at present, but the city is very sickly and numbers dying daily.*"

Although the President could not admit the possibility of the disease spreading in his own house, the servants sprinkled vinegar and camphor inside and set gunpowder afire outside, as recommended by many doctors to prevent the disease. Some doctors prescribed a vegetable diet and exercise as a way to keep the body healthy. Others advocated meat, potatoes, and a varied diet, rest and a cold morning bath. The Washington household tried them all. Nellie could hardly stomach all the greens the servants fed her, and she shivered after her bath, even with the towel wrapped tightly around her. In her grief for Polly she often wondered which was worse, the fever or the deterrent.

While the U.S. capital was still in Philadelphia, this red brick house served as one of several Executive Mansions.

The streets of Philadelphia were virtually deserted. Many had fled the city, and those still around cowered behind locked doors. During this time neither Nellie nor Little Wash could leave the Mansion to attend school, since the other children had already stopped going and the teachers had given up teaching. With so much disorder in the Mansion, Nellie found it impossible to practice her harpsichord.

The President soon let most of his secretaries go home, and, other than the servants going about their work, the Mansion was quiet. Nellie and Little Wash

spent hours staring out Nellie's window. Occasional pedestrians passing by walked quickly, holding wads of gauze to their noses to protect themselves from the contaminated air.

Too often Nellie heard the sound of wheels clattering on the cobblestones and was drawn to the window. She watched the open carts, usually driven by slaves, carrying piles of corpses. The carts paused at every house where there was a death from the fever. Afterward, they drove to large open pits where the bodies were buried.

Nellie's grandfather thought his place was in Philadelphia as a calm example to the people during this trying time. He would have stayed longer, but Nellie's grandmother, Martha, felt she had already suffered the loss of too many loved ones, and she was unwilling to risk the health of her two grandchildren. Martha convinced Nellie's grandfather that they must take Nellie and Little Wash away.

On September 10, 1793, Washington's servants hitched the team of cream-colored horses to the elegant, brightly painted carriage, and the family began their six-day journey back to Virginia and their beloved Mount Vernon. Nellie was reminded of their first trip to Philadelphia after her grandfather was elected. In each of the small towns they had passed through, people had waited to greet

George and Martha Washington sit for a formal portrait with Little Wash and Nellie. The artist also included William Lee, a house servant.

them. Now there were no people in the streets. She knew too many people were ill, and suspected those that weren't were scared and had shut themselves in their houses.

Although Nellie was still heartbroken over Polly's death, she was relieved to be returning to Mount Vernon. The eight thousand acres were open and free and stood right next to the Potomac River with its cold, sparkling waters, alongside which she and Little Wash could walk for miles and miles. Certainly life in Philadelphia, before the fever, had been full of adventures, but Nellie had felt closed in by the city and was sure Little Wash felt the same. They both looked forward to being with their dogs, Duchess, Doxey, and Vulcan, at Mount Vernon again; Little Wash couldn't wait to ride his horse and to chase the cattle and sheep grazing peacefully in the pasture, as he had in the old days. Nellie was excited at the prospect of renewing her friendships with the slave women at the mansion house farm. The slaves spun and wove the wool cloth from Grandpapa's sheep. Nellie had spent hours with them, and she missed their cheerful talk and comforting, sweet songs as they pulled the warp through the tightly stretched woof on the loom. And she looked forward to her grandfather's greenhouse, which was always filled, no matter the season, with a myriad of imported flowers and fine fruits and vegetables, including figs, grapes, limes, oranges, large English mulberries, and artichokes.

There wasn't much Nellie's grandfather could do to run the country from afar, but he did continue the business of designing the new Federal City. It was to be named after him and set in a wooded area twelve miles away from Mount Vernon. The city would include many governmental buildings and a large house for the Presidential family. The President made several trips to Washington, D. C., and the site of the new Executive Mansion. On October 13, Nellie's grandfather laid the cornerstone for what would eventually be the White House. It was originally to be a fifty-five- by eighty-five-foot mansion, the first of the new Federal City buildings. On his return, he told Nellie that the splendor of the music and drums and of the flying colors of the flag had made the ceremony a majestic and memorable affair.

The Washingtons stayed at Mount Vernon until the first frost ended the spread of the disease. On December 4, 1793, they returned to Philadelphia, and the President to his place as the nation's leader. Nellie and her brother went back to studying hard. Between the first of August and early November, death had claimed more than four thousand Philadelphians. But as the weather had finally turned cold and brittle, the newspapers reported the disease-carrying mosquitoes had been killed. Governor Mifflin of Pennsylvania called for a day of "Humiliation, Thanksgiving, and Prayer." Most of the city's citizens felt a great sense of relief.

But not Nellie. She stood at her window once again at 190 High Street and watched the horse-drawn carriages carrying elegant ladies back and forth from the hair salon, as if nothing had ever happened. Nellie knew, however, that her life was changed. With Polly Lear's death, Nellie had lost her dearest friend.

A Visit to Grandpapa's House

Thomas Jefferson "Jeff" Randolph looked forward to his grandfather, President Jefferson's, visits to Monticello more than anything else in the world. And now young Jeff and his family were going up to Washington, D.C., to visit the President. The winter season of entertaining was close, and President Jefferson wanted his family with him for the huge New Year's celebration at the President's House. Although it was the end of November, the air still had a crisp autumnal feel. Pushing and laughing, fourteen-year-old Jeff, his five sisters, and his brother, along with his cousin, Frances, piled into the carriage. While their excitement was contagious, his mother climbed in and reminded the children that it was a long ride from Monticello in Virginia, and they would have to be a little more calm.

Jeff endured three days of travel in all; two days of riding on a bumpy, dusty road, followed by one day of heavy rain and mud. While the carriage took them through a dozen small towns, Jeff tried to imagine his grandfather sitting at the long table in the comfortable study. His grandfather's letters always described the room and the table in detail, as well as how the study walls were now covered with maps, charts, and books, and how the library ladder reached the tall, mahogany bookshelves lined with more and more leather-bound volumes.

Most of his grandfather's correspondence was written to Jeff's fifteen-year-old sister, Anne, and to his ten-year-old sister, Ellen, but Jeff's sisters occasionally read their letters out loud. Jeff knew his grandfather missed all of them desperately and that, in their absence, his pet mockingbird was his constant companion. His grandfather had written that when he was alone, he would open the cage and let the bird fly free around his room. The room was full of plants and flower stands which held his grandfather's favorites: roses and geraniums. The bird would flit from one flower to another, finally lighting on the table where it would regale his grandfather with song. Sometimes it perched on his grandfather's shoulder and ate seeds from his lips.

One of the letters they received from Grandpapa long before they ever visited the Mansion had been written to Jeff's mother in 1801:

Facsimile of a letter to Thomas Jefferson from his granddaughter Ellen

Dear Martha,

Mr. Randolph writes me you are about to wean Cornelia; this must be right and proper. I long to be in the midst of the children, and have more pleasure in their little follies than in the wisdom of the wise. Here, too, there is such a mixture of the bad passions of the heart, that one feels themselves in an enemy's country. . . . It will be but three easy days' journey from you, so that I should hope you and the family could pay an annual visit here at least; which with mine to Monticello of the spring and fall, might enable us to be together four or five months of the year. I enclose for Anne a story, too long to be got by heart but worth reading. Kiss them all for me and keep them in mind of me.

Tell Ellen I'm afraid she has forgotten me.

As the carriage pulled into Washington, Jeff remembered their first visit, years before. His aunt Maria, who was still alive at the time, had remarked on the starkness of the city. In those days there were no hotels in Washington and only a few boarding houses scattered here and there.

Mostly he had seen miles and miles of vacant fields and waste land surrounding the President's House, but Jeff's grandfather had reminded them that Washington was still a new city.

Now, as the carriage drove through Washington, Jeff noticed that the city had grown. There were more buildings and even a few hotels. They passed other carriages. There was a hustle-bustle feel to the town that Jeff thought was new.

Dinner their first evening seemed to include all of Jeff's favorite foods: his grandfather's famous beef, marinated in salted olive oil for two hours before broiling and served with a delicious butter; steamed greens, fresh from the greenhouse; and french fried potatoes, which Jeff ate with his fingers. To finish off the meal, Jeff had a large bowl of ice cream wrapped in a pastry crust—a favorite recipe of his grandfather's French chef, Honoré Julien. The table was completely silent as he and the other grandchildren relished the creamy dessert.

Since Jeff's grandmother had died long before his grandfather became President, Dolley Madison, the wife of Secretary of State James Madison, was the hostess at those Mansion dinners where the mixed company could include diplomats or local residents. That evening, she had told the President that the public and press knew his grandchildren were in town and wanted to meet with them.

The Capitol as it neared completion during Jefferson's Presidency

Jeff was glad when he heard that she had told the reporters no. His grandfather's doors were always open to whoever wanted to see him in the morning on business; but in the evenings, he would not let the public intrude on his social hours. President Jefferson had little patience for small talk, which is why he gave only two enormous parties a year—one on July Fourth and the other on New Year's Day. Jeff's grandfather's other entertaining included small dinner parties with no more than eight guests at a time.

After dinner, Jeff begged his grandfather for a tour of the President's House. He wanted to see all the changes they'd heard so much about. Jeff and the grandchildren ran through the twenty-three rooms, which his grandfather had finally begun to decorate and furnish with them in mind. Jeff's laughter rang through the quiet, barn-like halls. He and his sisters were some of the first children to stay in this grand mansion, and his grandfather was always happier wth them around.

Jeff was particularly enchanted with his grandfather's inventions, or "conveniences," as Grandpapa called them. They were all over the house. In the dining room, surrounding the round table, were several dumbwaiters, triple-top tables that looked like shelves. When the President had guests, each of the dumbwaiters was filled with food, wine, and cutlery—everything a guest might need for the meal. In this way, there was no need during the meal for help from the servants, and the guests could feel free to talk about anything and everything they liked without the worry of any eavesdropping.

"Our walls have no ears," Grandpapa told Jeff proudly.

Jeff liked his grandfather's "cabinet," which was what the President called his office. It was roomy and warm with the two fireplaces both blazing, and through the large south-facing windows there was an unobstructed view down the Potomac River all the way to Virginia. Jeff's sister Ellen was intrigued with Grandpapa's long writing table. When she touched it, it flew open and Ellen saw all the things inside that her grandfather kept on hand when he studied late at night: a goblet of water, a decanter of wine, a plate of light cakes, and a candle.

"Is this where you write to me?" Ellen asked.

Grandpapa smiled and nodded while he picked up his favorite goose quill, which lay on the bronze inkstand. "And with this very pen," he replied.

Jeff chased his seven-year-old sister, Cornelia, into "the room with all the bones." Their grandfather had written to them about the new Entrance Hall. It was set aside for all of the specimens that the explorer Meriwether Lewis sent back from his expeditions for the President to study and display.

Out of the corner of his eye, Jeff saw Virginia, who had just turned five, trail off. She was in search of Grandpapa's mockingbird. Jeff giggled when he saw the bird following Virginia up the dark mahogany stairs when Grandpapa led them off to their beds.

Early the next morning, Dolley Madison arrived with her carriage to take Jeff and the children around the city. They needed new clothes for the New Year's Day celebration, so their morning began with a visit to the tailor. Jeff stood perfectly still while the master tailor, with his quick eye, sized him up and cut a waistcoat, knee breeches, and a fine velvet coat to be finished with exquisite embroidery. And for his sisters and cousin, there were long dresses with tight bodices and lace at the wrists. In the afternoon, Dolley made a quick stop at the toy shop, where Jeff bought a puzzle, a top, and books with his pocket money.

They went back to the President's House, where Jeff took his bath. A portable bathtub, which was really a large, painted tin bowl, was brought to the East Wing bathing room on the second floor by one of the servants. The bowl was lined with soft linen bath cloths to protect Jeff's skin from the hot tin. The water for the tub was warmed in kettles on the hearth of two coal-fueled boilers.

After dinner that evening, Jeff and his family gathered in the Oval Salon to listen to Grandpapa play his fiddle. The President played until there were hardly any flames left in the marble fireplace and the candles had all burned themselves out. Jeff fell asleep surrounded by the other children on the sofas and thick Persian throw rugs. In the morning when he awakened in his own bed, he knew that somehow his grandfather had carried him up the night before.

Finally, the New Year's Day open house that Jeff and the others had been waiting for was just days away. The President's House was a frenzy of activity. Jeff was in charge of bringing wood up from the basement and splitting and stacking it near each fireplace. A cow was slaughtered, butchered, and cooked slowly in the smokehouse. Wine was brought up from the ice house, and Jeff followed the servants as they carried up the trays, casseroles, and soup tureens.

Each of the oil lamps was filled, and extra wicks were brought up from the housekeeper's room. In fascination, Jeff watched the servants carefully clean the two glass chandeliers in the Oval Rooms on the first and second floors and put new candles in each one. On the day of the party all of these candles would be lit, as well as dozens of single candles carefully protected by elegant glass shades. He watched them clean the huge silver candelabras and fill them with new beeswax candles.

At dawn the day before the party, Jeff and Anne piled into the horse-drawn kitchen cart with the steward and rode off to the city market. The market was at the northernmost end of Presidents' Park, housed in one of the long sheds that had stored the construction workers' tools and materials while the President's House was being built. Now the shed was full of farmers, truck gardeners, hunters, and watermen. Jeff delighted in the noisy, colorful atmosphere. Soon their burlap bags overflowed with pheasant, venison, duck, oysters, squash, cabbage, potatoes, carrots, onions, mushrooms, and a dozen different cheeses. The steward steered them back to the cart.

When they arrived home again, Jeff was glad to be in the warmth of the clean kitchen with its good smells and big full pots. The great iron cookstove in the west end of the kitchen was already piled high with food. The servants had been cooking for the celebration for days, and every pot, casserole, fish kettle, tin mold, and pudding dish would be filled by the early morning of January 1. Jeff watched them lay out the fine white damask tablecloths and napkins on the tables in the large dining room.

Throughout his family's visit, the President had shielded his grandchildren

A busy marketplace scene in Washington, D.C., around 1800

from visitors, but at midmorning on January 1, the doors of the President's House were thrown open to the public. Jeff knew that everyone was welcome, no matter how rich or poor, as long as they were well-dressed for the occasion. People came from all over to pay their respects. They wanted to peer into his grandfather's private quarters and private life, and shake his grandfather's hand. They wanted to see Jeff's mother as well as Jeff and the other grandchildren.

There was still some snow on the ground, and it was cold. Jeff glued himself to the front window while military companies crowded up the freshly shoveled front walkway and into the house. The Marine Band played in the hall while all the guests entered.

Of course, all of Washington's "high society" showed up in their finest overcoats and brocades, their plumed hats and high-waisted dresses. But local farmers, dressed in their plain attire, and other residents were there as well.

Jeff and the other children gathered around the door, watching as people entered. Jeff was the first to see the large group of Osage chiefs and their attendant "squaws." They were tall and graceful. He stood close while his grandfather introduced the chiefs and explained to everyone how he had invited them to appear in their native costume.

The chiefs were dressed in deerskin moccasins, cloth leggings with embroidery, and fringes of colored beads. Their ears, noses, and the single tuft of hair at the crowns of their heads "were ornamented with a variety of foxes, bones, ivory

A view of the west front of Monticello, Jefferson's home in Virginia

trinkets in different shapes, curiously carved shells, and pieces of hard polished wood," Jeff's grandfather wrote. "The most gigantic men we have ever seen," he added.

When Jeff's grandfather introduced Ellen to one of the chiefs, Jeff watched his younger sister stare closely at the chief's face, which was in full paint of red, yellow, and green. His body was covered with blankets that wrapped gracefully around him but left his right arm free. When the chief put out his hand, Ellen blushed and curtsied. The chiefs were quite a contrast to Ellen in her velvet green dress and long flowing dark hair. Neither Ellen nor Jeff had ever seen a real Indian chief before.

Jeff's grandfather gave each of the chiefs a silver medal, which hung from a ribbon around their necks. The medal was a sign of friendship. In exchange, the Indians stepped forward with their gifts of blankets, jewelery, and tomahawks, which the President promptly asked the servants to display.

After all the introductions were made, Jeff crouched behind one of the large leather chairs while the other children went upstairs and left their grandfather and Dolley Madison to offer food and wine to the guests. From his hiding place, Jeff heard his grandfather tell a group that not long ago he had had the "aborigines," as he called the Indians, to dinner.

And on a number of occasions and regardless of what I fed them, they never seemed to look at either the food or cutlery with any curiosity. Until, once, during the last Fourth of July celebration, I brought the wine to the table in coolers filled with ice. On seeing the ice, one of the chiefs looked up at the others with doubt and surprise. He took hold of a piece of ice and when he'd felt the cold, he started to smile. Then the chief handed it 'round the table. As each one of the chiefs held the cold substance, they began to laugh. Soon enough the whole table was laughing.

Jeff's grandfather explained that when he had asked the interpreter why his guests were laughing, the chief responded by saying, "We now believe that what our brothers told us when they came back from the great cities was all true, though at the time we thought they were telling us lies, when they told us of all the strange things they saw, for they never saw anything so wonderful as this that we now see and feel. Ice in the middle of summer!"

Jeff grinned from his spot behind the leather chair as he pictured the Indians laughing and holding the ice. He wished he had been there to see and hear it all for himself.

Though the party continued until the sun had dropped behind the poplars, Jeff managed not to be found in his hiding place. Eventually he made his way to bed, and, before he fell into a deep sleep, he thought about how much he loved his grandfather, the President, and how happy he was to be able to spend so much time with him in the huge new Mansion. He wished he could stay forever.

1841–1845

JOHN TYLER

Diamonds and Ostrich Feathers

*I*t was summer of 1844, and twenty-three-year-old Letitia Tyler hung back from the lively celebration that had started in the Oval Blue Room and spilled over into the East Room of the White House.

It had been less than two years since her mother died, and Letitia remembered sadly that the last time the White House had been this full of people was at her mother's funeral. That night was so sad, and tonight was supposed to be happy, but she felt absolutely no joy in this occasion: the celebration of her father's marriage to Julia Gardiner, a woman only one year older than Letitia.

Letitia watched her three brothers and three sisters and wondered if they felt as upset about the marriage as she did. Then she glowered at the new "Lady Presidentress," as Julia was being called by the press. She noticed her father looked on quietly as her new stepmother picked up her full skirts with one hand and wheeled across the floor on the arm of what Letitia thought must be a reluctant partner.

Only three years before, when her father had acceded to the Presidency after President Harrison had died, he had sat all of his children down and told them how he felt they should act as children of the President. Letitia vividly remembered how he had warned his daughters that it was bad form to dance in public.

And now, in the presence of all of Washington's high society, this so-called replacement for her quiet, invalid, recently departed mother was dancing her heart out in front of Letitia's father.

Letitia looked across the room and saw her sister Mary's little son dancing about and clapping to the music. She wondered why Mary didn't stop him. Maybe it was because their new stepmother, dressed in a long white satin ball gown and gleaming headdress adorned with diamonds and ostrich feathers, was waltzing across the Blue Room into the East Room, indifferent to the fact that this was where their mother's coffin had lain for days. Letitia considered whether Mary even recalled their father's stern directive about such public displays. Moments later, Letitia watched the new Mrs. Tyler demonstrating a bouncy new Bohemian dance called the polka, while courtly ambassadors and astonished Cabinet members looked on. Letitia was utterly embarrassed for them all.

In the four decades since the capital city was founded, the trees had begun to shade the streets.

Letitia glanced at her two older brothers, Robert, twenty-seven, and John, Jr., twenty-five, and Robert's wife, Priscilla. Letitia liked Priscilla and would have much preferred she remain the White House Hostess as she had been for the year and a half that Letitia's mother had been unable to, as well as for the

twenty-one months after her mother's death. Priscilla hadn't even minded sleeping in the late President Harrison's room, in the very bed in which he had died. Letitia knew her mother had worried it would cause Priscilla nightmares, but it hadn't. Priscilla would have slept anywhere in order to help Letitia's mother, and Letitia admired the way Priscilla enjoyed looking after the youngest Tylers: Alice, who was now seventeen, and Tazewell, who was thirteen.

Across the Blue Room, Letitia looked for Dolley Madison. After her mother's death, Letitia and her brothers and sisters had stayed close to the "Queen Mother" as Dolley Madison was called. Mrs. Madison had been a good friend to Letitia's mother and had visited the fragile, paralyzed Mrs. Tyler often during her last months. Letitia had come to depend upon the wisdom of the widowed Mrs. Madison. When Letitia's eyes met those of Mrs. Madison, she gave the Queen Mother what she hoped was a polite and friendly nod.

Letitia thought of her sister Lizzie's wedding, just eight months before their mother died, and reflected on how different it had been from this event. Lizzie had had her wedding at the Mansion and her reception in the East Room with Cabinet members and their wives, diplomats and their wives, and family friends, including Dolley Madison. Letitia's mother had made one of her only public appearances in the White House at that wedding. Letitia remembered how her mother had worn a simple dress and how her face had been shaded by the soft fine lace of her cap. Mrs. Tyler had graciously received all the people who were led up to her, gently and sweetly stretching out her hand to greet friends, family, and dignitaries.

By comparison, the young Miss Gardiner and Letitia's father had exchanged quick, short vows in a dark Fifth Avenue cathedral, away from the eyes of both country and family and less than two years after her mother's death. They were the shock of the summer's social calendar. Neither Letitia nor any of her brothers or sisters had been invited. When Letitia had learned of the marriage, she had been stunned.

Letitia had heard that former President Adams said that her father and Miss Gardiner were the "laughing stock." She could certainly understand this since her father was fifty-four and Julia Gardiner was only twenty-four, thirty years his junior! Letitia felt angry with her father and jealous of his new wife, who was not only younger than Letitia's three older siblings, but was also a petite five foot three inches with an hourglass waist; Letitia was attractive, but big-boned with a heavy step. Julia had large gray eyes and raven hair parted in the middle

Julia Gardiner had been a friend of the Tyler children before she married their widowed father.

with a bun over each ear. If Letitia had looked closely, she might have noticed the similarity between Julia and the portraits of her mother at that age.

As Letitia watched Julia dance from one end of the Blue Room to the other end of the East Room, she remembered the first time she had met her.

It was winter, only four months after her mother had died. Her father had gone through his grief, reading and meditating. Books, magazines, and newspapers were scattered everywhere in his cabinet. Each evening in front of a blazing fire, he had read to Letitia and the others from his favorite writers: Dickens, Irving, Longfellow, and Thoreau. He had read to them from magazines and newspapers about what was happening outside the White House: how reformers were demanding free schools for both girls and boys, while others were demanding the abolition of slavery; how Morse code was making communication from far away easier; how steamboats and railroads were replacing clipper ships and stagecoaches; and how the cotton gin and the reaper were facilitating the agricultural industry. It was a period of creative thinking and commercial activity, but though the President read to them about the outside world, he found it difficult to keep up with the times.

Robert's wife, Priscilla, who was still acting as the Mansion Hostess at that time, had invited Julia and her sister to come for tea and a quiet game of whist in the Green Room. Priscilla had also asked Julia to bring along her guitar. Priscilla had hoped it would entertain her father-in-law and raise his spirits, for he was an accomplished violinist and enjoyed music thoroughly. Sure enough, that evening the President played his violin and even recited his poetry. Letitia had liked Julia then, for she had brought an evening of gaiety into her father's life, as well as her own.

But now, less than a year and half later, while the Marine Band's music swelled, Letitia found it utterly impossible to join the throngs of party goers congratulating the President and his new wife as the huge four-tiered cake was wheeled to the center of the Blue Room. Letitia's father, looking taller and more slender than usual, with his brown hair slicked back and his blue eyes shining, led his new wife to the center of the room. Together, the President and his First Lady faced the crowd and held a large shiny knife above the cake. As the knife came down and sliced through the cake, Letitia felt a rush of confusing emotions. She wondered how this new marriage would affect her life and the lives of those she loved.

Tad's Union Blues

By the time the horse chestnuts bloomed again in the summer of 1862 at the White House, nine-year-old Tad Lincoln was feeling a lot better. He leaned wearily against the headboard of his bed, while his gaze roamed blankly around the room. He stared at the marble-topped washstand with the fancy porcelain sink. The crisp linen towels hanging next to it were a reminder that he should get up and wash his face. But he didn't. Instead, he began to cry. The empty bed in the next room still reminded him that his older brother Willie was no longer alive. His parents had put Willie there, hoping the boys would get well more quickly if they were separated. Tad recovered, but Willie had died of typhoid fever.

Across the hall, Tad's devastated mother, Mary, had stayed shut up in her bedroom day after day since the loss of her middle son. When she finally did come out, she would never again go into either the bedroom in which Willie had died or the Green Room below, where he had lain in his coffin. She banned flowers from the White House because Willie had loved them. And she even canceled the Marine Band concerts on the South Lawn for the rest of the summer, because music was one of Willie's favorite pastimes.

Tad was lonelier than he could have ever imagined. When the brothers' unrestrained antics had gotten the two of them in trouble, Willie had been the

In this picture Willie Lincoln was about five years old. He died seven years later.

one to take the blame. Once they had climbed out a window, and the Mansion's flat roof had become a battleship for them to command. Their mother had seen them and shouted for them to come down, but they had ignored her. Another time, when a painter named Mr. Hicks had arrived from the East to do their father's portrait, both Tad and Willie had sneaked into his room, squeezed his paint tubes all over the wall, and rubbed bold streaks of paint on it with the palms of their hands. Each time, Willie had taken the blame for Tad, even though it was the boys together who were a team of trouble.

Willie had been studious, obedient, and always able to explain his way out of their mischievous crimes. And Tad had depended on Willie to interpret his lisp for all of those who had trouble understanding him when he spoke. Willie had known Tad was smart, even though Tad could barely read at all. Tad, two years younger, had hated work, was sometimes destructive, and loved to have fun, often at the expense of others. Behind his parents' backs, Tad had heard the servants and many of his father's close friends refer to him as "The Tyrant of the White House."

Tad left his room and made his way down the hall to the library, with its floor-to-ceiling bookcases filled with poetry, Shakespearean plays, and English novels. He hoped he might find his father there, reading, as he often did whenever he had a spare moment, but the library was empty. On his way down the grand stairway, Tad passed one of his father's secretaries, Mr. Nicolay, who in his heavy French accent said he was sure the President could be found in his office. Mr. Nicolay warned Tad, however, that his father was in the middle of dealing with some difficult issues regarding various Civil War battles and might not wish to be disturbed.

The President's office door was shut. Tad knocked on it with three loud, quick raps followed by two short bangs. Almost immediately, his father opened the door. "I promised never to go back on the code," the President told the six military officers who sat in front of his desk, all of them looking at Tad.

"What is it?" Tad's father asked softly.

"I want to take a drive," Tad replied, matter-of-factly.

Without a word to the officers, the President abandoned his meeting. Moments later, Tad and his father were settled in the Presidential carriage, accompanied on either side by mounted troops. Tad enjoyed the ride and didn't give a second thought to the officers or the important work that his father had left behind.

After Willie's death, Tad and his father went to town almost every morning. The number of shops had increased in the last few years and sometimes the two

President and Mrs. Lincoln sit with their three sons. Willie is seated, Tad is next to the President and Robert, the oldest, is standing.

would stop the carriage to look in at A. Stuntz, which had the best selection of all the newest toys. They would drive by the Capitol and then down Pennsylvania Avenue. In the dry season the road was barren and dusty, but when it rained, it became a sea of mud. The clash of sabers, the measured beat of marching men, and the shrill commanding voices of the officers were always in the air.

A. Stuntz store, where Tad and his father often shopped for toys

As the days pressed forward into autumn and then winter, Tad stayed by his father's side. The President tried to encourage Tad to play outside, but to no avail.

"No, no, Papa," Tad would protest, "I want to stay and see the people."

Tad listened intently as his father talked to army officers about military strategies and battles. He looked serious when his father was serious, and laughed when his father laughed. He was oblivious to the fact that he annoyed some of the men, who were tired of never being able to see his father alone. And it never occurred to him that some held back important information even when they did happen to find the President by himself. Tad didn't realize that some of the officers felt the President couldn't keep a secret from his young son.

Tad's father had always indulged him and his brothers, saying, "It is my pleasure that my children are free, happy, and unrestricted by parental tyranny." Now Tad took full advantage of his title as Tyrant of the White House.

Before his brother's death, Tad and Willie had been tutored in the Library upstairs. But the President now declared, "There's time enough for Tad to learn his letters and get pokey."

With a regimented school day no longer pressed upon him, Tad filled his time with pranks. Once, he turned a hose on one of his father's secretaries. Another time, in the middle of a White House tour his mother was giving, he drove his team of goats through the East Room, riding on a chair behind them.

On a quieter occasion, Tad decided to set up a table in the White House

Tad, July 1861, posing in Zouave uniform modeled after those worn by troops. Tad disfigured his own image with an inked-on mustache and goatee.

Entrance Hall to sell refreshments and take up collections for Civil War charities. Despite his lack of schooling, Tad knew how to make precise change and intently bargained with all of his father's callers.

Once when his brother Robert came home from Harvard University, and Tad saw him walking down the hall with their father, Tad raced toward them and jealously pushed Robert aside. He gave his father a fierce hug, ignored Robert, then dashed away. That night, while the President worked late, Tad fell asleep on the floor under his father's table. Tad awoke the next morning to discover himself in the trundle bed next to his father's huge bed. He knew that the President must have completed his work the night before, carried him down the hall, and placed Tad in the low trundle bed before wearily tumbling into his own.

Late in the fall of 1864, Tad and his father were to be photographed by Mathew Brady, one of the finest photographic artists of the time. Tad dressed up in his "blues," as he called his Union uniform. He was proud to have been given an actual colonel's commission by Mr. Nicolay, his father's secretary, along with a real uniform and a real sword, both made especially for him. While

Tad paraded around the White House, the President suggested that Brady and his assistant set up their equipment and darkroom in Tad's bedroom.

After the photo session, Tad returned to his room and found it inhabited by all kinds of equipment. Tad was so furious he shouted, "How dare you use my room! Who gave you permission?" Then, locking the photographers out and their equipment in, Tad stuffed the key into his pocket.

Though the President and Mrs. Lincoln had always allowed Tad the run of the house, this time his father did not smile. "Tad, do you know you are making your father a great deal of trouble?" the President said, holding out his hand for the key. Seconds later Tad gave it up.

That Thanksgiving the President received a huge turkey for the family dinner celebration. When Tad overheard the servants in the kitchen talking about what the dinner was to be, he begged, "Father, Father, someone is about to cut Jack's head off!" After his father proclaimed the turkey should live, Tad immediately adopted him as a pet and led Jack around the White House on a string.

In the last weeks of the Civil War, Tad went with his father to General Grant's camp at City Point, Virginia. It was the first time in many months that the President had left his desk. It was almost a vacation for Tad and his father. After they arrived at the camp, they rode together over the countryside on horses furnished by General Grant. The President rode Cincinnati and Tad rode Little Jeff, a smooth-paced little horse the general had captured from the stables of Mrs. Jefferson Davis, the wife of the Confederate President.

Tad and his father visited the surrendered cities of Petersburg and Richmond. They walked hand in hand through the still-smoking capital, buildings in ash at their feet and death everywhere. Tad was nervous and excited being in the rebel cities; he held his father's hand tightly.

Tad went everywhere he could with his father. In early spring, Tad was present when the President gave his final speech: "We meet this evening not in sorrow, but in gladness of heart. . . ." As he spoke, the President let each page flutter to the floor. Tad crawled in and out between his father's long, lanky legs to collect each sheet as it fell.

On April 14, 1865, while his father and mother were attending a performance at Ford's Theatre, Tad was watching a production of *Aladdin and His Wonderful Lamp* across the street. Half an hour into the production, the manager of the theater stepped out near the footlights and announced that

President Lincoln had been shot. For a moment there was absolute silence. Then Tad shrieked and ran up the aisle.

"They've killed him! They've killed him," he cried.

The following morning at 7:22 A.M., the sixteenth President of the United States died, leaving his son Tad once again devastated and alone.

1865–1869

ANDREW JOHNSON

---

ank Waits for
the Verdict

O n February 24, 1868, fifteen-year-old Andrew "Frank" Johnson, Jr., the youngest child of the seventeenth President of the United States, was shocked to learn that the House of Representatives had voted by an overwhelming majority to charge his father for "high crimes and misdemeanors."

"Impeach him!" was the cry heard around Washington, D.C. Frank knew impeachment meant his father could lose his position as President. He would need to prove his innocence during the upcoming trial in order to remain in office.

In the three years since the Johnsons had come to Washington, Frank felt his father had been a good President. He knew that after President Lincoln's assassination, his father had been left with a great deal of unfinished business. He had seen to it that the Thirteenth Amendment, which abolished slavery, had passed.

Lincoln had won the Civil War for the Union. It was now up to Frank's father to help reunite the land and make peace. Although the Southern states had seceded from the Union, Frank's father felt the country should forgive and welcome the rebels back. He wanted to make it easy for those states to resume their former place in the Union. But there were members of Congress who wanted to punish the South severely for seceding. They were afraid that the Democratic Party might become powerful again in the Southern states. These same men had opposed nearly everything Frank's father had tried to do.

The conflict between Frank's father and the Radical Republicans in Congress reached a crisis when the President fired the Secretary of War, Edwin M. Stanton. He was one of the leaders of the Radical Republicans and had been working hard to undermine Frank's father's work with the reconstruction of the Southern states. Congress had charged that the President had usurped its power. Congress wanted him out of office.

When Andrew Johnson's impeachment was threatened, his family had barely recovered from an exhausting renovation project left to them upon their arrival at the White House. After President Lincoln's death, his wife, Mary, had remained in her room in solitary confinement for thirty days, while idle visitors stole silver from the dining room and cut fringes from the curtains and furniture. It had taken Frank and his family a full year to turn the haunting shabbiness of the White House into a warm, livable home.

Frank had been put to work helping to paste fresh wallpaper and stuffing old cushions into new linen slipcovers. And his big sister, Mrs. Martha Patterson, had taken it upon herself to rid the house of bugs found in the furniture in the East Room, to scour away tobacco juice from around the spittoons, and to cleanse the grimy rugs, drapes, and upholstery.

Frank remembered how pleased his father had been at the sparkle and shine of the White House and how, after the monumental task, the President had called for party after party to celebrate the White House renovation and the family's real entrance into Washington society. When he closed his eyes, Frank could still hear the strains from the fifteen-piece Marine Band and the rustle of the taffeta skirts as the women danced across the wide carpeted floors covered with linen "crash" for dancing. All their new friends and the important governmental heads had been there.

But now the comfortable atmosphere and the festive receptions which Frank had so enjoyed came to a grinding halt. Even with his sister Mary and her three children, Martha and her two children, and his brother Robert around, the large house felt grim and quiet. His ailing mother, whose tuberculosis had begun to act up under all the pressure, kept to herself in her small bedroom upstairs and hadn't so much as a smile for Frank when he visited her daily.

It had been three agonizingly long months since the first vote to impeach Frank's father. Now, on May 26, while the Senate voted, Frank sat on the White House stairway between the first and second floors to await the decision. He knew his father hadn't really committed any crime other than opposing congressmen who were determined to control the direction of Reconstruction. But he was nervous and felt anxious for his father, who had kept mostly to himself since February. Congress was deciding his father's fate and, therefore, the fate of his entire family. What would they do if his father was convicted and removed from office? Where would they go? It would be, among other things, the greatest embarrassment of their lives. Tears came to Frank's eyes.

Every once in a while he glanced down at the open book in his lap. It was a brand new book, *Alice's Adventures in Wonderland,* and he would have liked to read it, but he couldn't concentrate.

In one of the basement rooms below, Frank's three nieces and two nephews were quietly finishing their lessons for the school day. He envied them their schoolwork, which might at least take their minds off the impending news. In another basement room, Martha was finishing up her duties in the small dairy. She loved cream and butter and had seen to the organization of the milking herself in order to provide for the family's needs. Each morning the "cowman" brought Martha two large tin pails of milk from her two Jersey cows grazing contentedly on the front lawn. Martha processed the milk, separating the cream. All of these normal daily activities seemed difficult for Frank to understand, under the heightened circumstances of the day.

Earlier that morning Frank had wandered down to the basement and into

President Johnson's eldest daughter, Martha Johnson Patterson, helped to run the household while her invalid mother was confined to her bedroom.

the room next to the dairy. He had watched the laundress and her assistant fold the clean sheets fresh from the clothesline. While they worked they were always listening for the sound of the little spring bells that would summon them to rooms all over the house.

Above him, on the second floor, he heard the quiet footsteps of the chambermaid as she went about cleaning and straightening the bedrooms. He had visited his mother in her second floor bedroom earlier and left her sewing in the chair nearest the large window as she did every day. He suspected she was probably even more nervous than he was.

Frank could smell the lamb chops and vegetable soup the cook had been preparing all morning for their dinner meal. He heard her quietly shooing her two small children from underfoot.

He finally closed his book and walked down the stairs to look out the window. Outside he saw the doorkeeper, the gardener, and the two guards sent over by the Treasury Department quietly stationed at their work.

He tiptoed down the hall. Frank saw that the door to his father's big office was ajar. He pushed it open a bit and saw his father standing in front of the large picture window facing Pennsylvania Avenue, his hands deep in the pockets of his dark cutaway jacket. Although his father had made it clear that he needed to be alone, Frank longed to say something; but words failed him. He quietly pulled the heavy mahogany door closed and turned to walk back down the hall.

When the front door suddenly burst open, Frank stopped in his tracks. An aide, followed by a guard and then the doorkeeper, flew in shouting, "He's acquitted. The President is acquitted!"

Frank's heart pumped wildly. He watched the aide take the stairs two at a

President Johnson's "big office" in the White House

time up to the second floor, while the door-keeper ran down the hallway and pounded on the door to the President's office.

"By a vote of thirty-five to nineteen . . ." Frank heard the doorkeeper shout excitedly. He knew it was only one vote short of the two-thirds majority needed to convict, but it was a victory nonetheless.

He headed upstairs. By the time he reached his mother's room, Mrs. Johnson had risen from her chair and had tears in her eyes.

"I knew he'd be acquitted; I knew it," she told the aide.

Within moments the whole family had pushed their way into the room, followed closely by all the servants. As they gathered around Frank's mother, happier than they'd been for months, the President appeared in the doorway. His face was flushed red with excitement.

"We need a party. A huge, noisy party to celebrate!" he said. And all at once his children and grandchildren surrounded him.

With the joyous news and his whole family together, Frank's eyes filled with tears. He wiped them away with his sleeve and, joining in the noisiness, started to laugh. "Yes! Yes!" he cried with an overwhelming sense of relief. "A party! A huge party!"

Overjoyed at his acquittal after the impeachment trial, President Johnson gave a large party.

Stumped by Stamps

For eleven-year-old Jesse Root Grant, the White House was the most exciting home he ever could have imagined. Although his two older brothers, Frederick and Buck, were away at college, and his sister, Nellie, was completely caught up with boys, dances, and parties, his father was around far more often than he had been since the Civil War had ended. They spent a good deal of time together, and there were always dozens of interesting people and a myriad of entertaining things to do.

During Jesse's first months in the White House, his father and mother made lots of changes. After their first dinner, Jesse and his family took a walk around the grounds. Jesse's father, President Grant, noticed there was a soldier keeping guard outside the dining room door. His father stopped the guard and asked him whether there were other guards posted. The soldier replied that there were two posted on the main floor and several more at the entrances and ground floor. His father, who didn't like the idea of the soldiers wandering around their home, promptly dismissed all the guards.

For awhile Jesse and Nellie attended school, though not with any great regularity. They both found more than enough to do just around the White House, and their parents permitted them to come and go as they pleased. For Jesse, there was a whole raft of boys who lived nearby, and soon they all became great friends. The boys came to visit often, not because Jesse was the President's son,

Toward the end of the Civil War and four years before he became President, General Grant and his family sat for this painting.

but because Jesse's playground was the biggest and the best around. In good weather, Jesse and his friends played in a vacant lot still on the grounds but just south of the Mansion, and when the weather was inclement, they played in the big, airy basement.

Jesse filled his days exploring the White House grounds, playing with his friends, and getting to know the thirty White House employees. He spent his evenings in the library with his mother, father, and Nellie. That is, until one of his father's friends purchased a small but powerful telescope for Jesse. From then on, every clear evening, Jesse spent hours on the roof of the Mansion. Soon his father began to accompany him. Together they studied astronomical charts and tables under the dim light of a lantern. The two of them would get so lost in the heavens, Jesse's mother would have to send a messenger to remind them it was time for bed. When his father was away on government business, Jesse invited his mother up to the roof. His mother's eyesight was poor, so Jesse would have to entertain her by recounting aloud his findings through the telescope.

Baine Dent was Jesse's thirteen-year-old cousin and one of Jesse's best friends. Jesse loved roaming the grounds with Baine and talking with the workers, especially Edward Burke, "the Furnace Man." Each day they saw him walking around the Mansion, attending to the open coal fires. He was a black man, and always dressed in plain, dark clothes. On Sundays, however, he would appear at the library door dressed in a double-breasted frock coat, which, when thrown open, showed a massive gold watch chain. He also carried a shiny plug hat and gold-headed cane.

Albert Hawkins, the coachman, was another of the cousins' favorites. The Mansion stables were Albert's domain. They were quite large, and he kept them meticulously in order. Many times Jesse and Baine found Albert eating his dinner from a tin tray placed on a stool, carrying on a running conversation with Jeff Davis and Rebbie, Jesse's horses, and Rosie, Albert's black-and-tan dog. Jesse often wondered if the horses or Rosie ever talked back.

Jesse's horses were both acquired by his father during the Civil War. When Jesse and his father had gone to the Virginia front during the war to meet with President Lincoln, Jesse had ridden Rebbie, while Tad Lincoln had ridden the gentler "Little Jeff."

Nellie and Jesse Grant several years before they lived in the White House

When Albert finished the last of the coffee in his tin cup, he would place a lump of sugar between his lips and call out, "Now, yo' Rebbie, yo' can't have none of this here." Rebbie would walk out of his stall and carefully take the lump of sugar from Albert's lips. Little Jeff, knowing that his turn was coming, would stamp and paw with impatience. Albert would place a second lump of sugar and say, "Now, yo', honey-baby, Jeff Davis, wouldn't take no sugar from Albert." And by that time the sugar would be in Jeff Davis's mouth. Jesse had to laugh at Rosie, for all the while she would be lying flat on the floor, intently watching Albert's mouth as she waited her turn.

Besides his horses, Jesse had a parrot, presented to him by the Mexican ambassador; two brightly colored gamecocks; and a succession of dogs, all of which seemed to live a short time and then die. One day Jesse received a magnificent large black Newfoundland. When this new

Horses Reb and Billy Button carrying the President's children to school, 1869.

dog arrived, Jesse's father called the Mansion steward. Jesse listened curiously. The President asked no questions and made no accusations.

"Jesse has a new dog," he said simply. "You may have noticed that his former pets have been peculiarly unfortunate. When this dog dies, every employee in the White House will be at once discharged."

Jesse's Newfoundland lived for the rest of his father's term, and he and Baine enjoyed the dog's company for years afterward.

During this same time, around 1871, Jesse and Baine were completely enthralled with stamp collecting. They found stamps everywhere, but were particularly fortunate when they combed the correspondence on the President's desk.

One day Jesse and Baine came upon an advertisement in the newspaper. A man who lived on Milk Street in Boston offered a large assortment of foreign stamps for five dollars. Five dollars was an extraordinary amount of money for a boy Jesse's age, and there was no way of acquiring so much except to save it. Jesse and Baine went without candy or soda water for weeks and weeks. Every cent of their pocket money was saved for the stamp collection.

When at last Jesse and Baine had the five dollars in hand, they composed a short letter and mailed it. Jesse calculated that the letter would arrive the next morning, and, with any luck, the boys would have their stamps in hand by the following day.

Several days passed, and the stamps didn't arrive. Jesse began to worry.

Finally, Baine pressed Jesse to talk to someone about the matter. So, Jesse approached his good friend Kelly. Kelly was a big-bodied and bigger-hearted member of the Washington police force, detailed on special duty at the White House. Next to his father, Jesse thought Kelly was the greatest man in Washington.

Kelly shrugged his huge shoulders. "Sure, ye better tell your father about it, Jesse," was his only advice.

And so, Jesse took the problem to his father.

"What do you wish me to do, my dear boy?" his father asked.

Of course, Jesse and his cousin Baine had been thinking a lot about this.

"I thought you might have the Secretary of State, or the Secretary of War, or have Kelly write a letter," Jesse suggested.

"Hmm!" his father said. "A matter of this importance requires consideration. Suppose you come to the Cabinet meeting tomorrow and we will take the matter up there."

General Grant, Jesse, and Mrs. Grant

Jesse was excited. He and Baine were certain that, with the help of the President and his Cabinet, they were bound to get either the stamps or, at the very least, the return of their five dollars.

It seemed a long time until tomorrow, so the rest of the afternoon was taken up "spying" on Jesse's mother, who, with the help of her servants, was moving furniture from one room to another. When the boys slipped into the Red Room, they caught Grandfather Dent sitting comfortably in an easy chair in front of the fire. Grandfather Dent lived with the Grants, and, on this particular day, Grandfather Grant happened to be visiting. The two old men had a running feud, and Jesse loved to listen in on their conversations. As the boys crawled under the long red sofa, Grandfather Grant came into the room.

"Accept my chair, Mr. Grant," Grandfather Dent said immediately, jumping up from his chair by the coal fire. Now Grandfather

Grant was known to have a hearing problem, and Grandfather Dent loved to use this to show how old and feeble the other man was. Grandfather Grant didn't hear the man's gracious offer of the chair and instead chose one of the stiffest and straightest chairs, drawing it up to the fire. Grandfather Dent hovered anxiously over Grandfather Grant, urging him to take the more comfortable chair. Grandfather Grant ignored him.

"Hello!" Mrs. Grant said as she passed through the room, carrying a large Persian rug supported by herself and two servants.

"You should take better care of that old gentleman, Julia," Grandfather Dent said in answer to her greeting. "He is feeble and deaf as a post, and yet you permit him to wander all over Washington alone. It is not safe; he should never be allowed out without an attendant."

And then, coming to life out of nowhere, Grandfather Grant replied, "Jesse, did you hear him? I hope I shall not live to become as old and infirm as your Grandfather Dent." Of course, that immediately gave Jesse and Baine's presence away, and Mrs. Grant laughed loudly as the two boys struggled out from their hiding place.

The next day, Jesse appeared at the Cabinet meeting at the hour his father had set.

"Jesse has a matter he wishes to bring before you, gentlemen," his father said.

Jesse told his story, ending with the suggestion that either the Secretary of State, the Secretary of War, or Kelly write a letter.

The Secretary of State said, "This is plainly a matter for the State Department to attend to."

The Secretary of War promptly said it was his intention as the head of the War Department to act at once.

Jesse listened attentively to the general debate, following which the other cabinet members all decided Kelly should handle the situation. As a group, the Cabinet members agreed Kelly's virtues and influence were solid. When the question of who should write the letter was put to a vote, most of the Cabinet voted for Kelly. When the decision was made final, Jesse went downstairs to find Kelly.

Kelly smiled at Jesse and promised to write the letter that night.

The letter read:

I am a Capitol Policeman. I can arrest anybody, anywhere, at any time, for anything. I want you to send those stamps to Jesse Grant right at once.

Signed, Kelly, Capitol Policeman.

A few days later the stamps arrived. The assortment of stamps well exceeded Jesse and Baine's expectations. Soon they were writing to all the American consuls asking for stamp specimens. And for a while, Jesse and Baine were philatelists to the exclusion of everything else. It wasn't until Jesse's mother told them they would have to write thank-you notes to all the ambassadors that their stamp enthusiasm wore itself out.

Their next project began at Christmas that same year, when Jesse and Baine decided to start a secret club. The boys approached four other boys. The President had given Jesse a small toolshed at the bottom of the vegetable garden, west of the house. Jesse immediately put the shed to use as a clubhouse and was voted the club's first President. They named the club the K. F. R. Society, and, so long as the club lasted, no one outside of its members was ever to know what the initials stood for. Jesse's father told him jokingly that it stood for the "Kick, Fight, and Run Society." Their membership continued to grow, and, as was typical with Jesse and his friends, just like other boys their age, there were many disputes and frequent fights.

During this same period of time, Mrs. Grant suddenly decided that Nellie, who had grown into a young woman, should now be accompanied to her dances by a male member of the family. Since Frederick and Buck were away at school, Jesse was chosen for the job. He hated having to dress up and was so afraid of girls that it didn't occur to him to participate in the dancing. He stood in a corner, glaring at everyone, and counted the moments till he would be able to go home. After the second or third dance, he began to nag Nellie to leave. Nellie tried to ignore him, but Jesse persisted in his nagging until Nellie had no choice but to go or risk a fight in public. When Jesse and Nellie arrived home, Nellie flounced off to tell their parents. Meanwhile, Jesse snuck up to his bed and made sure he was fast asleep by the time his parents found him.

Unfortunately for Jesse, as he grew older he had to escort Nellie to several other dances. It always caused him terrible embarrassment. But fortunately, the K. F. R. Society was his lifesaver, offering him the protection of good and close friendships throughout his stay in the Executive Mansion.

Easter on the White House Lawn

For weeks and weeks Fanny Hayes had looked forward to Easter weekend. She had picked out her clothes days in advance. Her favorite white dress with its brightly colored sash hung on the knob of the dark mahogany wardrobe door, while her matching shoes were laid neatly below. She bounced excitedly on the edge of her black-lacquered bed. Only one more day! She counted the days as she had while waiting for her tenth birthday. She could hardly wait until Easter Monday morning, when she could dress up in her white dress, fill her dark hair with pink ribbons, and be the hostess for the great Easter egg roll.

The White House was completely overcrowded with family members and old friends. When her nineteen-year-old brother, Rud, returned for several days from college, he was having difficulty finding a place to sleep.

"I feel fortunate just getting the soft side of the billiard table," he told Fanny and her seven-year-old brother, Scott. "There are cots in the hall, couches in the reception room, even billiard tables and bathtubs have to serve as beds," Rud declared. "Father has virtually no privacy. I have seen him retire to the bathroom and lock the door to prepare important state papers." Fanny thought the bathroom was a very strange place for the President to have to work!

On Sunday evenings, cabinet officers and senators joined President Hayes and his family in singing favorite hymns

And indeed, during this crowded Easter weekend, Fanny found that her father, President Hayes, frequently retired to his den, the most private of his offices, where he was available only to his family. Fanny was fascinated by the telephone in her father's den. She had never seen such a unique contraption. The National Telephone Company had installed it on a trial basis. It hung on a wall with wires extending out the east window and stretching to the Treasury building across the street. Her father didn't use it often because there were so few other people with telephones in Washington. It always startled them when it rang.

Fanny had been asked to remove her "baby houses" from the bottom of the stairway and to keep them out of the big hallway upstairs. They were in the way of the workmen who were patching and painting the Mansion in preparation for Easter. Fanny usually stayed out of sight between ten and twelve on Mondays, Wednesdays, and Thursdays anyway. That was the time when pushy visitors crowded their way into the East Room, the parlors, and the State Dining Room. Her oldest brother, Birch, called them "souvenir hunters." She had seen them take inkwells, as well as beads and pendants from the chandeliers, tassels and fringes from the curtains, and bits and pieces of everything that could be cut, torn, or carried off.

But this weekend the White House shone like polished crystal. It was filled to the brim with Fanny's brothers, aunts, uncles, and cousins. Winnie Monroe, who had been their nurse and family cook even back in Ohio, was cooking Fanny's favorite foods. Winnie was proud and excited about her role in the White House. She called herself the "First Colored Lady of the Land," which Fanny thought was entirely right.

Easter Sunday evening, with the table groaning under the heavy dishes of delicious food, Fanny's father asked one of the servants to bring him an apple. He carefully shined it on his jacket lapel, looked squarely into Fanny's eyes and then her brother Scott's, then turned his gaze up and down the table to all her cousins. Fanny watched closely as her father proceeded to peel and slice the apple. When he finished, he handed one slice to Fanny's cousin Maria and one slice to Fanny. Then, asking the others if they could catch, the President tossed them each a slice. Fanny laughed out loud when one of her cousins had a piece of apple stick square in the middle of her forehead. When Fanny later told Win-

Winnie Monroe with Scott and Fanny

nie about Father's tossing an apple slice to everyone at the table, she added, "All but Mother. She refused to take part in such 'undignified behavior.' "

That evening, before she went off to bed, Fanny stood with her brother Scott for a moment looking down the corridor to their schoolroom. Tomorrow morning was Easter Monday and neither of them would have school. Miss Rey, their teacher, would not come to the White House as she did on a normal Monday. *Everyone* would be on Capitol Hill. Since her father had reinstated the grand old tradition of the egg rolling, Fanny and everyone else in the White House was looking forward to it.

Fanny was too excited to go to sleep. As she lay there she wondered what tomorrow would be like. She had heard that years ago, on Capitol Hill, congressmen had gotten fed up with the egg roll, which, to them, meant lost and crying children, ruined grass, and trampled eggshells everywhere. Some of them had actually threatened that any child who showed up on Capitol Hill to roll even one egg would be thrown off the premises, even if it took all the policemen in town to do it. And last year, they had actually passed a law prohibiting the use of the Capitol grounds and terraces as "playgrounds or otherwise." She couldn't imagine why anyone would want to stop such a festive occasion as an Easter egg roll.

The next morning Fanny awoke and quickly got ready for the big event. When the time for the egg roll approached, she looked out the windows. She could see hundreds of children, each with a full basket of brightly colored eggs in hand, parading down the street toward Capitol Hill. All of them were dressed in colorful Easter clothes: the girls in their fancy dresses, white gloves, and Easter bonnets, and the boys in fine breeches.

Fanny and Scott with their mother and cousin George (far left)

Ready to leave, Fanny eagerly ran to join her father and mother in the den with Easter basket in hand. She jumped at the shrill ring of the telephone so early in the morning. From her father's conversation on the telephone and then with her mother, Fanny knew that the call was about the egg roll. There had been trouble at the Capitol, and the children and their parents had been turned away, her father said. The President looked at his wife, questioningly.

"Bring them here," Fanny's mother said softly.

For a moment, Fanny was confused. The grounds of the White House were flat while Capitol Hill was steep. Seconds later as she watched out their windows, her eyes grew wide. Within minutes the front lawn of the Mansion filled with hundreds of young children like herself. Her confusion quickly turned to excitement. In another moment, she and her brother were out on the lawn in all their Easter finery, laughing, yelling, and playing with the other children.

Fanny had forgotten that she was to act as hostess for the egg roll. Instead she delightedly rolled her own eggs down the lawn alongside all the other children— rich and poor, black and white. She was having a fabulous time!

When a boy who looked about fourteen suddenly snatched a basket of Easter eggs away from a tiny child who was sitting near her, Fanny called out.

"Stop him!" she yelled, as the boy fled through the front gates and down the street with a group of children running after him. Finally the police captured the young boy, and Fanny was pleased when he was made to return the basket to the little child.

Later that evening, when Fanny and Scott sat around admiring their brightly painted eggs in the kitchen of the White House, the President asked them if they'd had a good time.

Fanny looked up and smiled. "Never better, Father. Never better."

1881

JAMES A. GARFIELD

Summer of Sadness

It has been a very drowsy, lazy day—Papa has been moved for the first time, into another room, while the men have taken up his carpet and given the room a thorough cleaning out. He stayed in the front room until five o'clock sleeping quietly nearly all the time; his temperature rose two degrees, but after the doctors dressed the wound, it went right down again. How happy I will be when Papa gets well.

—From the diary of Mollie Garfield, Age 14, July 28, 1881

Just four months earlier, Mollie Garfield and her four brothers had moved into the White House. Her father had been inaugurated as the twentieth President of the United States on the cold, blustery day of March 4, 1881. Mollie remembered there had been a huge sleet storm the night before, but the day of the inauguration, when they'd taken their places on the outdoor platform built over the steps of the Capitol, the sun had finally come out, and the slushy streets and bedraggled flags that waved above them had begun to dry.

In the first days of her father's Presidency, the house was always full of people. Mollie's best friend, Lulu Rockwell, was a constant visitor, as was former President Hayes's daughter, Fanny. When Mollie gave a tea party in Fanny's honor, all of her girlfriends came and they had great fun together.

Mollie and Hal Garfield, at the top of the tree, pose with their cousins.

Mollie had been allowed to continue at Madame Burr's school with all of her old friends. Each morning she was glad when she could close the Mansion door behind her and walk the several blocks of cobblestone streets to her school. With her schoolbag thrown over her shoulder and her dark hair pulled back tightly in a ponytail, she enjoyed the red-brick townhouses, the horse-drawn streetcars, and the cabs. And she liked being on her own and away from the antics of servants, little brothers, big brothers, and her mother and father.

Mollie had been looking forward to her first summer at the White House. And despite the fact that the temperature in Washington was becoming hot and miserable, she enjoyed playing with her friends in the shade of the big trees that surrounded the Mansion.

Mollie's new life was shattered when her father was shot on July 2, 1881, as he waited at the Sixth Street station in Washington for the train that would take him to join his family at the beach in Elberon, New Jersey. She now hovered anxiously in the hallways, and, no matter how hard she tried, she couldn't sleep. After a few days when it began to look like her father might recover, Mollie allowed her hopes to rise.

She knew that now, if her father lived, when school started in the fall there would be police guarding her every step. Her life would be different: restricted, maybe even lonely. But right now, none of that seemed important. She only wanted her father to regain his health.

During this time, Mollie found solace in writing in her diary. Her days now seemed so full of her father that she appreciated the quiet time alone.

Friday, July 29. It has been a very pleasant day today; Papa is still slowly improving. Lulu came down about 11 o'clock and we went over to bid Miss Pauline [one of Mollie's teachers] *goodbye. She, her sister, and Margaret Merrick are going up to Portland, Maine. After we came away from there, I went up and staid with Lou until 4 in the afternoon. Came home and took a pleasant ride with Mrs. Sheldon* [one of her mother's friends and the wife of General Sheldon] *and Mamma. Dear Aunty Sheldon went away this evening. Such a lovely woman.*

Tomorrow we are going down to Mt. Vernon with Mrs. Stevenson and all the Soldiers' Home [the presidential summer cottage located just outside of Washington] *crowd. Haven't quite decided whether I shall go or not, all depends how Papa is tomorrow. Retired at 20 minutes of 10.*

Mollie was still wide awake the next night when she got home, so she carefully penned the day's activities in her diary.

Saturday, July 30. Such fun as I have had today—at 9½ this morning, all of us including Mr. Brown [the President's secretary, who would later marry Mollie], *went down to Mt. Vernon* [the usual way of going to Mt. Vernon in those days was by steamboat] *with the Stevenson party, and oh we had a gorgeous time. The weather was just perfect, and we all rushed around generally. Poor Mr. Brown had to lie down for a little while because he felt the motion of the boat and it made him ill. He amuses me so. When we reached the home of our great ancestor, we looked all around, and then fell in to eat, and oh how I did eat! We staid there until 1 o'clock and came back home. When we got to Washington, we all rode out to Soldiers' Home and spent a delightful evening, reaching home about 9 P.M. Oh, I have had just what I call a jolly good time. But I fear I won't get to sleep because I drank coffee.*

The next day Mollie was able to write:

Sunday, July 31. Papa is doing splendidly.

I fooled around all the morning with Don [Lulu's brother and a friend of Mollie's brother James] *and Jim; they found some kind of compressed air machine* [which had been used to help relieve their father's discomfort], *and it made a horrible noise when it became full of air. So these boys saw Col. Rockwell quietly sleeping and took it right up by his bed and let it go off with a "phiz." In the afternoon Mamma, Don, Jim, and I took a walk around the grounds; went down and fed the fishes in the fountain at the back of the house. Came in and lazed away my time until nearly 11 when we retired.*

Mollie's hopes continued to rise as her father improved.

Monday, August 1. The new month has started out splendidly; Papa doing gloriously; improving all the time.

This morning I went down street with General Swaim and Buffy to get a "philopeno" [Filipino] present for Don; I picked out a little old man trying hard to keep on a high flying horse. It is very odd, and Don likes it very much, so he says. Got a very nice letter from May Mason, must answer it soon. In the afternoon Mamma, Hal [Mollie's oldest brother], and I took a drive, around the city in a very roundabout way. Papa is sleeping now though the doctors had a fight to get him to sleep tonight.

We lazed around until 10 when Mamma and I retired.

For the next several weeks, Mollie's papa seemed to improve steadily, and she felt free to leave the house. She swam at the Washington Swimming Pool with her brothers and her girlfriends; went on picnics with Don and Lulu and Nellie Windom, another close friend; played billiards at the new billiard table in the Mansion; and made trips down the Potomac on the *Dispatch*.

As the time drew closer for Hal and Jim to go off to Williams College in Massachusetts, Mollie helped them to mark their names on their clothes with indelible ink and to pack their trunks. The family had several farewell dinners until finally, on September 5, her brothers left.

The summer was still scorching and the air thicker and muggier than ever. Mollie wished it would be more comfortable for her father.

As the President, although still ill, was improving nicely, it was decided that Mollie, her mother, and the President's two doctors could accompany him in "the cars" [the train] on September 6 to the cooler and more pleasant New Jersey coast. Mollie was delighted. Her father's doctors felt the sea air would do him

Crowds gather as the Presidential train sits on its newly laid track by the seaside in Elberon, New Jersey.

President Garfield is loaded into railway car for recuperative trip to New Jersey

good. She knew her father had been looking forward to the trip all summer. Mollie had overheard him telling her mother, "I have always felt that the ocean was my friend and the sight of it brings rest and peace."

To make the trip as easy as possible, a special track was built up to the North Portico from the Sixth Street station. There was a specially arranged bed in a separate car for Mollie's father. As the train sped across Maryland, Delaware, Pennsylvania, and New York, and into New Jersey, Mollie saw crowds come out everywhere to watch them go by. It was a journey of two hundred and thirty-eight miles, and it took just under seven hours. Mollie was hopeful that the coast would help her father to recover quickly.

Mollie found lots to do when they arrived in Elberon and didn't write in her diary for some time. Her father seemed to be getting better, then unexpectedly took a turn for the worse.

She finally wrote of his illness three weeks after they arrived.

> *September 29, 1881. It has been a long time since I wrote in my diary and I feel like a different girl now. We all thought darling Papa was on the sure road to recovery, but we were all mistaken, even the surgeons didn't know anything about the wound.*
>
> *We got Papa out of hot Washington and took him to Elberon, where for the first*

few days he seemed to rally, but it was merely temporary, and so after suffering with all the tortures that any human being could possibly do, he died at 10:35 P.M. on the 19th of September 1881. Dear little Mamma bore up with heroic courage and bravery until the very last, and then she was completely broken hearted. . . .

It is something really beautiful to see how much the people had gotten to love Papa through all his sickness. One thing touched me especially; while we were carrying Papa's remains to Washington, we came past Princeton; the whole college were down at the depot, and had strewn flowers all along the tracks, and after the train had passed the station, the boys all rushed on the tracks and gathered up the flowers to keep as a memento of that sad, sad day. At every town and railroad crossing the people were standing, some bareheaded, and all with very mournful faces. Baltimore was a sight to be remembered. People had come from miles around, with all their children, even their babies, hardly expecting to see anything but the train; the car Papa was in was draped inside as well as outside, in the deepest mourning.

I dreaded most of all reaching Washington. As we came near, that 6th Street Depot loomed up and I was afraid we would have to go through it, but it had been arranged that we got into a carriage right at the back of the depot and were driven as rapidly as possible up to Attorney General MacVeagh's. Their house was high up from the street, so it was like being out in the country when we were in the yard. I never knew until then what a dear, good woman Mrs. MacVeagh was. I forgot to say that Hal met us at Elberon, and came on to Washington; dear old Jim wasn't able to accompany him, on

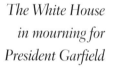

*The White House
in mourning for
President Garfield*

account of an attack of malarial fever, so he consented to wait for two or three days and met us in Cleveland.

It seemed rather sad to think that we were leaving Washington for good, though I don't think I should ever be satisfied to live there again.

It was almost a month after Mollie and her family had moved from Washington, before she was able to write in her diary about her father's burial.

Sunday, Cleveland, October 25. Well, I must tell about Papa now. They took him down to the Main Square where there had been erected a magnificent catafalque, in which they let Papa lie in state until they should take him to the cemetery. The whole city was draped in mourning, even the shanties where the people were so poor that they had to tear up their clothes in order to show people the deep sympathy and respect they had for Papa; I believe if he were able to look down on us, he would be deeply touched to see how much everyone loved him—the Democrats as well as the Republicans, and the South fully as much as the North—not a thought is given to the difference of opinion in politics. All persons are friends in this deep and great sorrow.

Grandma, Irwin [Mollie's younger brother], *and I went in the carriage following Mamma's. The procession was seven miles long, double row. It took us two hours and a half to reach the cemetery, and there we put dear Papa in the receiving vault which was covered almost entirely with ivy; there was a carpet of flowers clear from the hearse to the vault; there we saw the last of darling Papa, a sweet resting place for such a noble, brave, and loving man.*

The White House Gang

Four-year-old Quentin Roosevelt was getting increasingly bored and impatient. His older brother Archie's room had been off limits for days. Quentin watched the doctor come each morning and again every afternoon. He overheard the doctor tell his mother Archie had measles. Quentin had only briefly glimpsed the awful-looking red spots that covered his brother's body before his mother told him he could no longer go in Archie's room. The doctor said they weren't dangerous, but Archie could go blind if they didn't keep his room dark.

Archie was Quentin's best playmate, and Quentin was getting lonely. He spent a good portion of every day sitting outside his brother's door, waiting for him to get well. One morning, after a good deal of thought, it occurred to Quentin that nothing would help his brother get well more quickly than to see his little calico pony, Algonquin. So without a moment to lose, Quentin raced down the long, carpeted stairway, out the huge double doors of the White House, and around back to the stables. He nagged one of the coachmen to help him, and, together, they managed to lead the bridled pony from the stable all the way into the White House basement without running into a single officer or guard. Quietly Quentin and the coachman led Algonquin into the elevator and

Quentin (on the end) and Archie line up with the White House Police Guards.

up to the second floor. It was a long walk down the corridor and finally into Archie's room, but when Archie saw Algonquin, he laughed out loud. Quentin knew the mission had been a total success, and, fortunately for him, the pony hadn't had any "accidents" along the way. Now he was certain his brother would get well more quickly.

His brother did get well soon, and they were once again tearing around the White House. Quentin was used to running free at Sagamore Hill, their summer home on Long Island, so he took full advantage of the spaciousness of the Mansion and romped and roamed wherever he liked. He and his brother spent hours racing up and down the hallways past the officers and guards, the congressmen, and the secretaries. One of Archie's favorite pastimes was to slide down the long staircase on one of the sterling silver trays that he took from the kitchen. Quentin would laugh and try to do the same, but he was never as good at it as his brother. Quentin preferred the fun of parading around on stilts, surprising one of the White House tour guides as he went "stilt walking" through the East Room.

Quentin loved it when the whole family played hide-and-seek. Everyone who took part in the game enjoyed it, even his oldest sister Alice Lee and the President, when he wasn't busy. Every closet and corner of the White House was open territory for that game. No room was sacred.

When he wasn't romping through the White House with Archie or playing hide-and-seek with his family, Quentin had a huge menagerie of pets to entertain him. There was Bill, a horned toad; a half dozen guinea pigs including Father Grady, whom Archie had named only to say later, "Uh, oh, Father Grady has had some children"; Eli Yale, a blue Brazilian macaw; Emily Spinach, Archie's garter snake; Fidelity, Ethel's pony; Jonathan Edward Bear, who later became the property of the Washington Zoo; Josiah, a badger; Manchu, Alice's spaniel; Peter, a bullterrier who distinguished himself by biting through the trousers of French Ambassador Jules Jusserand, the family's dear friend; Slippers, a cat with six toes on one paw; dozens of dogs ranging in size from terriers to a Chesapeake retriever; and of course, Algonquin, Archie's horse.

Theodore, Jr., with Eli

The entire family enjoyed their pets, and, much to Quentin's delight, his father let the children keep almost anything they could find. They took their pets *very seriously.* When Quentin's favorite mongrel dog, Skip, was killed by a car at Sagamore Hill, the entire family and staff went out to the back garden where they held a funeral and a burial at which a proper eulogy was delivered.

No matter whether the Roosevelts were at the White House or Sagamore Hill, at four o'clock every afternoon, everybody stopped work and paid attention to the children. His father called it "the Children's Hour." Although *The Wind in the Willows* was his father's favorite book, and he read it to the children often,

President and Mrs. Roosevelt seated with their children (from left) Quentin, Theodore, Jr., Archie, Alice Lee, Kermit and Ethel

Quentin preferred to hear about his father's wild adventures in the West. "Tell us about the ranch!" he would beg, and soon Father would be deep into his stories about the "bully" herds of cattle that he and the other cowboys had rounded up each evening.

The Children's Hour usually ended in a romp with his father, Quentin, and the others tumbling and wrestling enthusiastically or engaging in a pillow fight.

One evening at dusk after the Children's Hour had finished, Quentin and Archie sneaked out of the White House. They scurried around the grounds until they found the lamplighter lighting all the electric lamps around the White House grounds. Keeping out of sight, Quentin and Archie followed him until he had finished his job. They waited patiently under a bush until he was long gone and dusk had turned the sky to the blue-black of night. Then the two of them shimmied up the posts and began turning out each and every light. They were only satisfied when the entire White House grounds stood in complete darkness. When they had just about finished the job, one of the watchmen caught them and sternly marched them home.

Grand dinners in the State Dining Room followed by "Mother's riotous musicals" were special times for Quentin. He loved to watch his mother sing and dance, waving her arms and swinging her legs, her voice strong and loud. Often Quentin, Ethel, Kermit, and Archie would sneak out to sit in their pajamas at the top of the stairs and watch the gaiety and the colorful panorama of the reception. But someone would always start to giggle, and soon they would be falling all over each other and down the stairs until their mother would have to quietly slip away to shoo them back to bed.

The year Quentin was five, his father went on a five-day bear hunt in Mississippi and Louisiana. The reporters that followed his father into the wilderness wrote stories that kept Quentin and the rest of Washington informed of the President's activities. The newspapers reported that the President had come upon a bear that was quite old, and he didn't have the heart to shoot it. Quentin laughed when told how the bear awakened, looked at his father as if he were no more than a tree stump, and then sauntered off.

Shortly thereafter, Morris Michtom from Brooklyn, New York, made a toy bear out of a golden plush material, reportedly because he was so pleased that President Roosevelt had not shot the bear. When Quentin's father returned from his hunting trip, Mr. Michtom sent the bear to him, asking if the President minded if he named the toy after him and called it a "Teddy Bear." Quentin's father was delighted and so were Quentin and the rest of the family. Naturally, Quentin wanted one of the bears for himself.

When the heat of the Washington summer arrived, Quentin returned to Sagamore Hill with his family. For him it meant real freedom—freedom from the city, the officers, and the guards at the White House. It meant fresh air, long runs, riding, swimming, fishing, clamming, lots of cousins, and longer hours of fun and frolic. And even though his father brought his White House secretaries, and there was a daily parade of congressmen and senators from Washington to speak with the President, Quentin's father would still quit his work at four o'clock every afternoon to spend time with Quentin and the others.

President Roosevelt and his boys

Quentin also loved summers best because he knew he and his brothers would get to go on their annual camp out with their father. Every year his father reminded them of the rules: "First, a boy must be able to dress himself; and second, all ills, including mosquito bites and drenching rain, must be dealt with cheerfully."

As Quentin grew older, he helped prepare for the camp out more and more. He filled four or five boats with blankets, axes, frying pans, cutlery, and a kettle. And when he was old enough, Quentin and several of the other boys rowed the five or six miles to the camp. When they docked, Quentin cheerfully made up his tent amid the buzzing mosquitoes. Then he and the others would go for a swim while their father prepared dinner. Quentin was certain that those meals at their annual camp outs were by far the best meals he ever ate. After supper in the evenings, the President would regale them with tales of his days riding the range out in Dakota, while Quentin and the others relaxed by the fire.

In the later days of the Presidency, when Alice was off and married, and Kermit, Teddy, and Ethel were away at school, the school term found only

Quentin and Archie in the White House. Around that time Quentin helped form "the White House Gang," an insider's club that included Archie, Charlie Taft (the Vice-President's son), and six other boys. Because Quentin was strong, forceful, and full of fun, he was their trusty leader. They all shared a clubhouse, a secret handshake, and good meals. There was no end to the trouble the boys caused both while Quentin's father was in office and again when Charlie Taft's father became President.

Once the White House Gang was riding in the backseat of a streetcar making faces at everybody who passed. The President's carriage pulled up beside them, and Quentin and the others began to direct their face-making toward Quentin's father. When the streetcar stopped for a moment in traffic, Quentin's father leaned forward in his carriage and said, "Quentin Roosevelt and you other little rascals, I think you have very nearly succeeded in making a fool of me in public. I had the idea of asking you to ride with me. On second thought I have concluded that it is entirely too dangerous for me to be seen with you." Pretending anger, the President pulled his hat lower on his head, then motioned for his driver to pull his carriage away from the streetcar. When he was out of earshot, he burst into raucous laughter.

1909–1913
WILLIAM HOWARD TAFT

A Peek Backstairs

Although Lillian Rogers did not actually live in the White House, she knew all about the Taft family. She knew that President Taft was a large man and that he had a reputation for eating huge portions of food. For breakfast he sometimes ate an eighteen-ounce steak if he wasn't dieting. She heard all about the huge bathtub that had been made especially for him.

Lillian had also heard about Mrs. Taft and how beautifully she dressed. She was known to be quick-witted and energetic. When it came to having her own way it was said that Mrs. Taft was a "doer." Although for many years the White House had been run by a male usher, when the Tafts moved in, Mrs. Taft hired a female housekeeper. Between her and the housekeeper, the White House was always shipshape, full of flowers and guests. There were luncheons, afternoon teas, and large gracious dinner parties.

Robert, nineteen years old, and the eldest son, was in his junior year at Yale. The only daughter, Helen, was seventeen and studying at Bryn Mawr. Lillian knew that they wrote to their parents often, and when either of them was at home, there was a huge celebration.

Charlie Taft was eleven. During the Roosevelt administration, he had been a good friend of Quentin Roosevelt's, and so when the Tafts came to live in the White House, the staff already knew he was full of fun.

Lillian's mother, Maggie, who was the upstairs maid in the family quarters

President and Mrs. Taft (seated) with (from left) Charles, Helen, and Robert

at the White House, returned home every evening and relayed story after story about the Tafts to Lillian and her brother Emmett. Most of the stories were about Charlie.

Charlie's father, the twenty-seventh President of the United States, had been inaugurated on a cold, snowy morning, and Charlie had taken Robert Louis Stevenson's book *Treasure Island* to read just in case he got bored listening to his father's inaugural address. But Lillian's mother said by all accounts she had heard, Charlie hadn't even opened his book that day.

If only Lillian could have been at the White House more often to witness for herself the hilarious antics that Charlie pulled. One of the capers she had heard about and had found most amusing was when Archie Roosevelt and Charlie had been caught under the table in the State Dining Room tying together two guests' sets of shoelaces.

It was obvious that Charlie was active and inquisitive. He loved to ride around in his father's automobile, a White Steamer, which was long and black-lacquered with a convertible top, and he liked to chase Pauline, the milking cow that grazed on the White House lawn.

Lillian wished she were free to do some of the things Charlie did, such as chasing Pauline. But even if she'd lived in the White House, she wouldn't have been able to. When she was only six, Lillian had had polio. She had been left handicapped and had a heavy brace on her leg. Running around just wasn't an option for her. Her mother told Lillian about Charlie's older sister Helen and the beautiful pink silk dresses she wore out in the evenings. Lillian said to her mother, "Someday I will walk without a brace and dance in a 'HelenPink' dress when I grow up."

Lillian thought it must be terribly fun and interesting to be one of the "First Children" instead of only the Head Maid's daughter. One of the many things that excited her were the telephones. Lillian didn't have a telephone at her house. Not only did Charlie have lots of telephones to use all over the Mansion, he even got to operate the switchboard sometimes, answering the telephones for the operators. One night, Lillian's mother brought home a pair of brown wool knickerbocker trousers for Emmett, who was ten, and told Lillian how she had come to have them.

Lillian's mother had found Charlie holding down the switchboard while the

Charlie's favorite spot was the front seat of the Taft family car.

PRESIDENT TAFT AND HIS FAMILY
IN THEIR WHITE STEAMER

operator had gone to lunch, so she had stopped just behind the door to eavesdrop.

"Certainly not," she had heard Charlie say firmly to someone on the other end. There had been a pause; then Charlie had spoken again.

"Somebody has been giving you misinformation. . . . An absolute denial . . . Well, if you want to quote me exactly, you may say that I said the rumor is false."

"Later that day," Lillian's mother told her, "I heard Mrs. Taft questioning Charlie as to what the conversation was all about. And at first Charlie didn't want to say. 'Purely personal,' was all Mrs. Taft could squeeze out of him." Lillian raised her eyebrows, wondering what it was Charlie could have been keeping so

Charlie and his sister and father are ready for a ride.

secret. Her mother continued, "[Mrs. Taft] was suddenly afraid, I think, that something was going on that the President should know about. When she took the story to the President, he got Charlie to admit that [a] reporter on the telephone wanted to write something about the fact that he still wore knickerbockers.

"Charlie was so embarrassed. He's almost twelve and his legs are beginning to look quite long. He so much wanted to wear long trousers," her mother concluded with a sigh. Lillian grinned as she pictured Charlie trying to look grown-up in his knickerbockers.

Her mother went on to tell her that a family council had been held immedi-

President Taft's extra-large custom-size bathtub was large enough to fit four workmen.

ately, and finally the President, Mrs. Taft, and even Charlie's sister had agreed that it was high time to fit Charlie with long trousers.

Although Lillian didn't spend nearly as much time at the White House as she would have liked, the stories her mother told her and her brother at dinner every night gave Lillian a wonderful idea of what life in the White House was really like. Each time Lillian went with her mother to work, she longed to run into Charlie, Helen, or Mrs. Taft, or even the President himself. But, mostly she'd had to be content with her mother's stories.

One evening Lillian's luck changed. As was the case each day, Lillian's mother would leave the White House late in the afternoon and come home to Lillian and Emmett for dinner. After dinner, she had to return to the White House briefly in order to turn down the President's covers. On this particular evening after dinner, Emmett had gone over to a friend's house. Lillian's mother was afraid to leave her alone when she went back to the White House, so she took Lillian with her.

While her mother arranged the bed linens, Lillian waited in the President's bedroom. Her mother went to turn on the dim electric lights in the other bedrooms, an important and prestigious job since electricity was still so new and unfamiliar. Some of the other servants were too afraid of being shocked to touch the switches.

"Don't make a move," Lillian's mother told her as she hurried out, "and don't touch the bed, and I'll be right back to get you."

It took all of Lillian's reserve not to immediately jump up to have a look in the President's bathroom. She would have liked to see the huge bathtub for herself.

But since her mother had told her not to move, Lillian didn't move a muscle.

Before her mother returned, a very stout man came into the room. To Lillian, he looked big and jolly, and he beamed down at her. Lillian knew he must be Charlie's father, the President. She had thought she would be scared of him, but she wasn't at all.

"Well, well, what have we here?" he said. "Are you the little ghost of the White House I've been hearing about?"

"No, I'm not a ghost," she assured him. "I'm Maggie's little girl, and I'm not supposed to be here."

The big, friendly man laughed. "Then let's pretend you're not here."

"All right," Lillian said, relieved. "Just don't tell Mama you saw me."

And as far as Lillian knew, the President never did.

1923–1929
CALVIN COOLIDGE

Cal Kicks Up His Heels

*D*id my father take dancing?" Calvin Coolidge, Jr., asked his mother, with a mischievous twinkle in his eye. Cal was tall for fifteen and blond. According to everyone he looked just like his father and the rest of the Coolidge side of the family. But unlike his father, who was rather quiet and serious, Cal always wore a smile. In this way he was more like his mother.

"No, he never took dancing," Cal's mother admitted with a sigh.

Outside the subdued and rather conservative Coolidge White House, America had erupted into the era of the Charleston, and Cal's mother wanted Cal to be part of it. Center-parted hair, slicked down and shiny like patent leather; snappy hats; saddle shoes; and raccoon coats were the fashion for young men. Women's skirts were shorter than ever before, falling just below the knees. They wore silk stockings and fake jewelry, and it seemed every woman, no matter how old or young, was bobbing her hair. The times were exciting, and people were confident and carefree. Thousands of soldiers had returned home from World War I, having witnessed firsthand the bloody fighting in Europe; they now thought they understood the value of life and vowed to get the most out of it. Everyone wanted to own a telephone, a radio, a phonograph, a washing machine, and, most of all, a shiny "Tin Lizzie" Model T Ford. Cal's eyes sparkled when he thought of the excitement waiting for him just outside the Mansion. But dance lessons! That was going a bit too far, he thought.

Cal's mother wanted Cal and his brother to get a taste of this new era, while Cal's father wanted to protect them from the eccentricities that came with living in the White House. Cal knew his father wanted his sons to have as normal and sedate lives as possible.

"Well, if my father never took dancing, I don't need to," Cal said decidedly to his mother.

"No, we don't want to go to dancing school," his older brother, Butch, added.

Cal and Butch (left) play pachisi with their parents.

"Try it anyway," their mother urged. "Then you can decide for yourselves."

Finally persuaded, Cal began to practice dance with Johnson, a young black doorman who loved Louis "Satchmo" Armstrong and his mighty New Orleans trumpet. Cal's teacher was a great talker and a fabulous dancer. He told Cal stories about New York's Harlem; Coonie's Inn and the Cotton Club; the Broadway theater; his "flapper" lady friends; and even about some of his friends who concocted "bathtub gin" at home, while others visited the secret saloons, called speakeasies, where they could drink illegally.

As Prohibition had been instituted a few years before, there were theoretically no alcoholic beverages in the White House or anywhere else in the country. Cal found Johnson's tales fascinating and fun; he enjoyed the way the outside world was beginning to seep in through his dance instruction. In the South, Johnson told him, he had friends who lived in the country and worked by the light of the moon distilling the corn whiskey known as moonshine. There were mobsters, like Chicago's Al Capone, who smuggled alcohol into the country and battled with the police and rival gangs.

There was so much outside the White House that Cal wanted to know more and more about. If it weren't for his older brother's and Johnson's stories of life in the "real" world, Cal might have found life at the White House rather dull. Although he felt close and comfortable with his mother and respected his father, his father was "boss," and for both boys what their father said was as irreversible as the Ten Commandments.

The President rarely smiled. Once or twice Cal had overheard the servants refer to the President as "Smiley," obviously poking fun at his father's stern, tight-lipped expression. Cal knew his father did have a sense of humor, but it was often caustic and sometimes at the expense of others. He remembered the time his father had once pressed all the buttons on his desk in the Oval Office, ringing the complicated

Calvin Coolidge and his sons working on a hay wagon.

bell system from one end of the White House to the other. As maids, doormen, and housekeepers appeared from all directions in his office, his father had merely smiled and said, "Just wanted to see if everybody's working."

Cal remembered the day he found out his father had been made President. He had been working in a Connecticut tobacco field for the summer when the news arrived that President Harding had died suddenly and Vice-President Coolidge was to succeed him.

"Isn't it great about your father being President?" his employer had asked him, and given him a congratulatory slap on the back.

"Yes, sir," Cal had replied, then swung a huge tobacco bundle down at his boss's feet. Hardly looking up, Cal added, "Where do you want this tobacco put?"

A fellow laborer had grabbed his arm and said in a loud whisper, "President? If my father had just become President I wouldn't be bundling tobacco."

Cal had looked up and said with a smile, "If my father were your father, you would."

Mrs. Coolidge with Rebecca

After moving into the White House, Cal soon discovered that the public had its own ideas about what boys growing up in the White House needed. Someone sent him and Butch a couple of lion cubs. Cal had fallen madly in love with them. He had gotten down on the ground with the cubs and roughhoused for hours. For days he had tried to talk his parents into keeping them, but to no avail. Soon the cubs had been shipped off to the Washington National Zoo, along with most of the other animals that continued to arrive from time to time. The one wild animal that didn't go to the zoo was a raccoon named Rebecca.

Rebecca also became the President's special pet, and Cal and his father built her a little outdoor house. Rebecca stayed in her shed at night and wandered the White House halls during the days. She unscrewed light bulbs and unpotted palms. She was even friendly with the two White House cats, Blackie and Tiger.

Blackie loved to use the elevator and would sit quietly waiting for someone to come and push the button to open the door for him. One morning Cal, who was on his way to play tennis, opened the door. Blackie immediately jumped on the elevator seat. When Cal got off on the first floor, Blackie stayed on the seat and continued to ride up and down in the elevator, entertaining everyone, including the President, who said, "Morning Kitty," in a friendly tone. "Wish I could spend the day riding up and down in this thing."

Cal also enjoyed the collection of dogs at the White House. His mother had a pair of white collies, Prudence Prim and Rob Roy. Paul Pry was an Airedale who got his name from snooping around the White House grounds, and there were also Calamity Jane and two chows named Timmy and Blackberry.

"Rob Roy is the boss," Cal explained when anyone asked which of the dogs was the leader. "He shows the others what to do and he keeps everyone in a state of terror."

And Cal was right. Immediately after his father went to work, Rob Roy would herd the gang of dogs like wild animals on a run through the halls. The maids would run for cover. Cal found it sometimes hazardous, but terribly amusing.

"I should inform your father," Maggie Rogers, the upstairs maid, told Cal more than once. But Cal knew she wouldn't. Whenever the President or Mrs. Coolidge was around, Rob Roy always behaved like a perfect angel.

Cal's first Christmas in the White House was spectacular. He and Butch had both gone off to the Mercersburg Academy in Pennsylvania in the fall and were expected home from school by Christmas Eve. Cal's mother had scheduled a dance for them and invited sixty young couples. The White House was festively decorated, with fir wreaths, red satin bows, and colorful packages everywhere. Earlier in the week, Cal's family had been presented with a huge spruce tree from Middlebury College in Vermont. The tree had been sent by express train and hand delivered to the White House by a group of people associated with the Society for Electrical Development, his mother told him. It had been placed outside, directly behind the White House. It was to be the first National Christmas Tree.

Several days before, a crew installed the underground electrical cables connected to the tree, and a thousand small white lights were then woven through its branches. Like everyone else, Cal stood by quietly and watched.

Cal's father had agreed to push the button that would light the lights on Christmas Eve. There was a buzz of activity and cheerful talk everywhere, while carolers gathered outside and a radio crew arranged themselves. After his father pushed the button that lit the tree, the air exploded with "Oohs" and "Ahhs" and applause, and the night rang out as the carolers sang everyone's favorite Christmas songs.

Afterward Cal and Butch gathered with their friends in the State Dining Room for the most lavish food Cal had ever seen on one table. When Cal and the others had stuffed themselves, the party moved to the East Room, where the Marine Band struck up a familiar tune:

Yes, sir, That's my baby,
No, Sir, don't mean maybe,
Yes, Sir, That's my baby now. . . .

Cal grabbed a partner and was instantly out on the dance floor. As he kicked up his heels, swinging his arms high in time to the music, his summer in the tobacco field seemed a long time ago.

Special Guests

*I*t only took three months to build the dressing rooms and long, narrow indoor swimming pool at the White House, but to Sistie it seemed like a lifetime.

On March 14, 1933, the New York *Daily News* and forty-one other newspapers around the country announced a campaign to raise money to build a pool for Sistie's grandfather, the thirty-second President. He had been paralyzed from the waist down by polio, and swimming was the only kind of exercise he could do. The time was the Great Depression, and most people were worried about jobs, where their next meal would come from, and even, for some, where they would live. Still, thousands and thousands of donations for the pool came in. Frequently a whole family would send in one dollar or an entire class of school children would chip in their pennies to make a twenty-five or fifty-cent contribution.

Each day, Sistie and her younger brother, Buzzie, the two blond darlings of the White House, stood and watched the workers dig up the Western Terrace. (The Western Terrace had been built by Thomas Jefferson, turned into a greenhouse under President Pierce, and used as a billiard room under President Grant.) Sistie's mother had told her that when the pool was finished, she would be able to swim in it with her grandfather. Sistie could hardly wait.

Sistie Roosevelt (left) and Diana Hopkins (right) stand in the front row of a Franklin Delano Roosevelt family Christmas portrait.

To Sistie, the White House was a luxurious and glamorous place to live. There were teas in the afternoon, informal cocktail parties in her grandfather's study in the early evening, and dinner parties in the State Dining Room every night. Hundreds of people were always rushing about, and everyone, including the maids and kitchen staff, paid lots of attention to Sistie and her brother.

From what Sistie had overheard, her mother had caused an awful scandal by divorcing her father and bringing her and Buzzie to live in the White House. But Sistie enjoyed seeing her aunts, uncles, and cousins as they came and went to and from the Mansion. Her youngest uncles, Franklin and John, drifted in and out, bringing friends home from college for lively parties in the East Room. They told her tales of life with their father, her grandfather. She loved her Uncle John's story about inauguration night, when he drove up to the White House gates in his cherished roadster and the guards wouldn't let him in. "Go on," they had said. "No son of the President of the United States would be driving such a junk heap."

"And so," John would say, "I had to sleep in a hotel lobby that night!"

The story always made Sistie laugh, thinking about her uncle being locked out of the White House.

"Another thing that was locked were the refrigerators," John told Sistie. "In the first months, Brud [Franklin, Jr.] and I wanted food before bed. We'd come into the kitchen and find the refrigerators locked up tight as a drum. We were starved and there was nothing around to eat!" After that, their mother had always seen to it that there was plenty of food available for her "night owls."

Sistie's day always began early. She and Buzzie would burst into their grandfather's bedroom around 8:30 A.M. and jump on his bed.

"Good morning, you rascals!" her grandfather would say, usually with a cigarette dangling from the side of his mouth. As Sistie jumped and bounced, the President would playfully grab for her feet and arms, trying to bring her down.

She and Buzzie were the only ones who were ever allowed to interrupt their grandfather's morning routine. One morning, when she and Buzzie were bouncing on the bed and their grandfather was on the telephone, she shouted, "He's my grandfather!"

"No, he isn't, he's mine!" Buzzie shouted back. They argued back and forth until finally their grandmother had to remove them so their grandfather could carry on his telephone conversation.

Sistie loved the upstairs Oval Room, which was her grandfather's cluttered study next to his bedroom. She loved the big overstuffed chintz chairs, the walls covered with her grandfather's collection of paintings of ships, and his books piled everywhere. Many of the books were for children, and Sistie would lie on the lion-skin rug for hours going through Dickens, Tennyson, and Kipling. Kipling's *Just-So Stories* was her favorite.

Her grandfather's desk was covered with trinkets and bric-a-brac: a small ship's clock; several little china donkeys; porcelain bears; a glass squirrel; and a

President Franklin Roosevelt's desk

cotton-stuffed, white muslin elephant, which was Sistie's favorite. She would make up games and move the animals all around the desk. Sometimes the ashtray and Camel cigarettes, which were always on the desk, doubled as a barn and fence posts.

Also on the desk was a small black-iron Scottie which resembled Fala, their grandfather's little pointy-eared dog, and a mechanical automobile with a puppet called Charlie McCarthy at the wheel. Sistie was allowed to play carefully with everything, but the toys and trinkets sent by his admirers were special to her grandfather, and always had to be returned to his desk.

One day, Buzzie and his mother stopped by the office just after Sistie's grandfather had received an electric flag on a stand.

"Plug it in, Anna," the President told his daughter, and a tiny electric motor caused the flag to wave gently. Buzzie fell instantly in love with it and was overcome with excitement. Sistie knew what was going to happen, and, sure enough, several hours later his grandfather had the flag delivered to Buzzie's room. Their grandfather was a generous man who shared his toys.

After breakfast, Sistie liked to play either on the roof, where her grandmother had installed a teeter-totter and a playhouse, or on the grassy lawn where she and her brother would race their two retrievers, Jack and Jill. Sistie had a sandbox, a metal slide, and a jungle gym to play with, but mostly she liked to take turns on the old fashioned swing that hung from one of the huge old trees.

Sistie and Buzzie ride with their mother and grandfather.

One day Buzzie walked up to Sistie all grins and giggles. He told her he'd had an adventure. After Buzzie had fed his dog some of the leftover pudding from his plate at lunch, he looked around for someone to play with. But Sistie had been in the garden, and everyone else was busy. Buzzie had been left alone and was bored stiff. So he had walked down one of the ramps built for their grandfather's wheelchair, and out the front door, where a large shiny black automobile was parked in front of the house. A Secret Service agent

Sistie and Buzzie throwing snowballs in front of the White House in 1939.

sat lazily on the car's hood. Buzzie pulled himself up tall, announced to the agent that his grandmother was sending him on an errand, opened the door, and got in the car, and away they went.

"Where to?" the agent asked Buzzie after driving a couple of blocks. Buzzie looked at the agent in the rearview mirror and hesitated. When he finally spoke up he gave directions that were so vague the agent immediately knew Buzzie had duped him and quickly headed back to the White House. By the time Buzzie finished the story, Sistie was laughing hilariously, wishing she'd thought of something like that.

But her chance for a similar prank ended when her mother remarried a short time later and they all moved out. Despite periodic visits from Sistie and Buzzie, the White House seemed very empty without the regular comings and goings of children, until eight-year-old Diana Hopkins moved in.

------

*A*fter Diana's mother's death, she and her father were invited to live at the White House. Diana was lonely and unhappy, but the excitement of living in the White House helped her forget her sorrow for a time.

But there were worries in the White House too. Europe had been fighting the Second World War for two years, and Americans feared a military attack, perhaps on the White House itself. Diana's father was personal adviser to the President, so she heard that the size of the White House police force had been doubled. Police had been moved into the basement of the East Wing and stationed on the roof of the Executive Wing. During her first weeks there, Diana observed all the added precautions taken to protect the President and his home. There were blackout curtains hung at the windows and heavy wooden crates placed over the two huge mirrors in the lobby to keep splintered glass from falling out if a bomb should hit the house. There were machine guns on the East and West Terraces, which made Diana extremely nervous. Several times a week a fire bell would clang loudly and everyone—the President, his family, the staff, and Diana—would grab their gas masks and squeeze into the cramped room underneath the North Portico until the all-clear signal came.

This was a frightening time for everyone, and especially for Diana. While she lived at the White House, hardly anyone besides the housekeeper and maids was around for her to talk to. She was lonely, and walking the police-guarded paths that surrounded the White House, often carrying her favorite doll under her arm, made her feel like she was in a jail.

One of President Roosevelt's greatest fears was fire. Because of his handicap, he was afraid he would be trapped in the house, unable to escape.

One night Diana was awakened by the wild clanging of bells. Her father had warned her about the nighttime fire drills, and also had told her about the special chutes that had been installed all over the third floor, where Diana's and her father's bedrooms were, and the underground escape routes in the basement of the White House. But thinking that it might be a real fire, she threw off her covers and raced barefoot out of her room. She had decided that no matter how afraid she was, she would slide down one of the chutes. Fortunately her father was at the window before she arrived, and he picked her up and held her close, explaining that it was only a drill. After the drill was over, he tucked Diana snug in her bed.

For a while, Diana was free to use the swimming pool whenever she could convince someone to take her. Once, while her father was ill and in the hospital, he wrote to her: "I hope you are swimming every day and have given up the use of the water wings."

Diana had the most fun when she had someone her own age to swim with—either one of the President's many grandchildren or, occasionally, a friend of her own who was allowed to come to the White House. Unfortunately this fun didn't last very long, because soon America entered World War II. Like all the outside gardens and the front lawn of the White House, the glass-enclosed pool became off-limits to Diana and most of the rest of the household.

Despite the fearful and protective atmosphere during Diana's years at the Mansion, she had the opportunity to meet many of the famous people who were invited to visit the President. Once she was able to have a long talk with Winston Churchill, the Prime Minister of Great Britain, who was visiting for Christmas. Churchill brought her a doll, which made her feel very special. On Christmas Eve, while the President read Dickens's *A Christmas Carol,* just as he had done every year since his own children were small, the Prime Minister sat next to Diana and they enjoyed the story together.

Other British visitors were King George VI and Queen Elizabeth. Diana was extremely excited at the prospect of being able to meet a real king and queen. She wondered if the Queen would be wearing a long flowing dress and a jeweled crown. And should she bow or curtsy? What should she say to a king and queen?

Diana Hopkins, Fala, and Winston Churchill at the White House, January 3, 1942.

That evening, when the King, in his dark military uniform with the shiny brass epaulets, and the Queen, in her long, spangled dress and her sparkling tiara a blaze of diamonds, entered the hall, Diana gasped in amazement. She curtsied gracefully to each one and then smiled brightly.

"Did the Queen look like you expected?" Mrs. Roosevelt asked her later.

"Oh, yes! Just like someone out of a storybook," Diana answered.

Later that evening Diana's father was waiting for her downstairs. She could hardly contain herself when she saw him, and, forgetting her White House manners, she ran toward him. At the top of her lungs she shouted, "I have seen the Fairy Queen!"

1953–1961

DWIGHT D. EISENHOWER

Howdy Doody, 3-D Glasses, and Ike

*I*n 1953, soon after his grandfather was elected thirty-fourth President of the United States, Dwight David Eisenhower II visited the White House for the first time. Not only did his mother and two little sisters, Barbara Anne and Susan Elaine, come along, but even his father was with them. David's father, John, had been a soldier fighting in the Korean War when David's grandfather was elected. Apparently Mr. Truman, the outgoing President and a friend of the family, had felt it important enough for the newly elected President's only living son to be present at the inauguration. So he had sent for John in Korea. David was as excited to have his father home again as he was to stay at the White House.

Not long after they arrived at the White House, five-year-old David ran through every single room on the second floor. He poked his head into his grandfather Ike's cherished study, where the President loved to paint when he wasn't working. He barged into his grandmother's "pink fluffy" bedroom. Everyone else called her Mamie, but David called her Mimi. Then David took the stairs two at a time to the third floor, where he had been told he and his sisters had their bedrooms and a playroom. He was amazed at just how many bedrooms, living rooms, dressing rooms, and bathrooms there were at his grandparents' new home.

Eisenhower family portrait

"Mimi!" he shouted to his grandmother. "Why do you live in such a big house?"

But David soon got used to the enormous Mansion and the dozens and dozens of people who helped his grandparents manage it. He and his family loved to visit his grandparents as much as his grandparents looked forward to having them.

During his grandfather's Presidency, television was still relatively new and few families had sets. David enjoyed watching on the small black-and-white set in his White House playroom. There were four programs he would never miss: *Lassie,* about a collie that always managed to save its owner from all kinds of trouble; *The Mickey Mouse Club* with its Mouseketeers (David loved to march around the White House singing "M-I-C-K-E-Y M-O-U-S-E"); and *Howdy Doody,* where Claribel the Clown always made David's baby sister Susan howl with laughter when he used his horn to "talk." Friday nights at 8:00 *Ozzie & Harriet* had him glued to the set. David even liked the commercials, which advertised newfangled items like garden hoses, frozen foods, Jell-O, and Gerber baby foods, which made feeding Susie much easier for David's mother.

When David visited the White House, the events of the outside world filtered in through the small black-and-white box. President Truman was the first President to use television as a way to speak to the people of the United

States about what he was doing in Washington, and President Eisenhower was also to make good use of it. During David's grandfather's administration, the war in Korea ended, and it was the first time in years that the country was at peace. Unemployment was low. People were less cautious about spending money on toys, vacations, and all kinds of other luxuries than they had been in a long time. Jonas Salk had discovered a vaccine for polio which would soon come close to wiping out the disease.

TV introduced David to Disneyland, a brand-new amusement park, which had just opened near Los Angeles, California. The Hula Hoop was the biggest rage in toys for children. Musical variety specials showed him a hip-shaking, gyrating singer named Elvis Presley. Sporting events were broadcast, showing him baseball players, including Mickey Mantle, who was the Most Valuable Player for the American League in 1956 and 1957. Dr. Seuss was also in the news. He had just published *The Cat in the Hat,* which became an overnight success.

But the news was not always good. The American Medical Association had proven that smoking causes cancer. Los Angeles smog had been analyzed and found to cause major crop damage. And the hydrogen bomb, which was found to be 600 times more powerful than the atomic bomb dropped on

Watching television was an Eisenhower family activity.

Hiroshima in 1945, was continuing to be tested in the Nevada desert.

Televsion was not the only form of entertainment for David. He loved comic book heroes: Superman, Beetle Bailey, and Li'l Abner were his favorites. David liked nothing better than to watch Saturday matinees at the White House's private movie theater, which featured such exciting thrillers as *Bwana Devil* and *House of Wax.* The movie industry had developed 3-D movies to compete with television. Glasses with special red-and-blue cellophane lenses made the images on the screen appear to be three-dimensional. David tried to resist the urge to duck when that happened, but usually he flinched in spite of himself.

David's playroom in the Solarium was a perpetual mess. The shelves, tables, and floors were always littered with the newest toys. Every month hundreds and hundreds of toys arrived at the White House. It seemed that all the toy manufacturers wanted the President's grandchildren to be the first to try their products. His mother tried to hide them, but David knew her hiding places, and he usually managed to coax her into letting him have the gifts.

Lionel Trains sent David an electric train, which ran around tracks set up all over the room, and another of his favorite toys was a rocket ship control board. He spent hours sitting at the control center with lights flashing, buzzers buzzing, and Morse code key controls clicking. He even had an interplanetary

There were always presents when visiting the White House.

plane and a radar scope to pretend he was on a space ship, heading toward Mars.

Sometimes David and his sister Barbara Anne played together with her home soda fountain, which included a real battery-powered mixer, little cans of chocolate syrup, straws, an order pad, menus, and recipes. And both of them knew that if they didn't share with Susie, there would be trouble. Ike and Mimi ran a pretty strict household, and their rules included sharing.

David watches his grandfather play his favorite game.

David wore his hair short in the crew-cut style popular for most boys of the 1950s. People told him that he was the spitting image of the President, and he liked that. He could look deadly serious one minute, and then flash an electric smile in the next, just like his grandfather.

David had a special relationship with Grandfather Ike. In the late afternoons when David was visiting, his grandfather would come to the playroom, and the two of them would go out to the putting green on the South Lawn. David had his very own made-to-size clubs, with chromium shafts. While the President practiced his swing, David would imitate him. He knew that when he was good enough, his grandfather would take him to the Burning Tree Country Club, where the golf course was as large and as beautiful as a park.

When the President appeared at the door of the Solarium, David would jump up to greet him. They had a special greeting where they extended their hands in a courtly manner and bowed low from the waist while they exchanged handshakes. Striving to be highly dignified, David sometimes bowed so deeply he almost fell over.

David and his grandfather had another trick that neither Mimi nor David's mother appreciated. It worked best when David was wearing his navy blue blazer buttoned carefully over his set of holsters and cap pistols. No one could see the pistols, but David's grandfather knew he was wearing them because they had practiced doing this a dozen times. They would greet each other casually, then

President Eisenhower with Barbara Anne and David; Vice-President Nixon with Julie and Patricia

suddenly the President would clap his hands loudly. David would tear open his coat, pull out his monster-sized cap gun—a model of an old frontier six-shooter—and shoot several times. David and his grandfather thought it was the greatest trick ever. But the noise from the cap guns usually scared Barbara Anne and Susan Elaine half to death, sending them crying to Mother or Grandmother Mimi.

Three years after his first visit to the White House, David's mother gave birth to a baby girl, whom they named Mary Jean. David was amazed at how tiny she looked in his father's arms. But before long Mary Jean was big enough to ride in the electric car that David raced around the White House drive. His other two sisters, now seven and four, would pedal their shiny tricycles as fast as they could after David and Mary Jean, all four of them racing down the bumpy roads of the south grounds.

Sometimes David and his sisters would get lucky and talk one of the housekeepers into coming to supervise them while they swam in the pool. David would park his car out front, do a fast change into swim clothes, and then practice belly-flops and cannonballs off the edge of the pool, drenching anyone who was near. Often, his grandmother Mimi would bring David and his sisters peanut-butter-and-jelly sandwiches or egg salad with pleny of mayonnaise to enjoy by the pool.

In the summer evenings, David's grandfather Ike liked to cook out. The grown-ups ate steaks and baked potatoes and the kids had hamburgers and hot dogs. David and his family would watch the sky darken as the sun set and the stars came out. Dessert was usually a cake made from one of the many box mixes that Mimi collected and David liked so much; the cakes were topped with pink frosting and mint green flowers around the borders.

On occasion, Vice-President Nixon would bring his two girls over for a movie or a meal. During Grandfather Ike's second inauguration, eight-year-old Julie Nixon had a conspicuous "shiner" that captured David's attention. He stared at it the entire afternoon, wondering where a girl could possibly have gotten a black eye.

When his grandfather's second term ended, David was twelve years old. He was terribly sad to be leaving the White House, and before they moved their belongings out, he wrote, "I will return! Dwight David Eisenhower," on several scraps of paper and hid the papers under rugs and behind paintings. David took a long look around before he climbed into his parents' station wagon. He was absolutely certain it would not be the last time he was at the White House.

Caroline's White House Schoolhouse

The date was September 25, 1962. Caroline Kennedy was excited to be back in the White House and in school. Today she was a first grader! Although Nannie Shaw, who had been with her since the day she was born, tried to restrain her, Caroline ran ahead down the wide second floor hallway and leaned eagerly on the up button of the elevator. The long and fun-filled salt-water-and-sand summer by the beach in Hyannis Port, Massachusetts, was over. It was still hot and humid in Washington, and, although she would miss playing with her thirteen cousins every day, she knew they would visit her. They always did, no matter where Caroline lived. All she could think about now was the shiny new lunch box clutched in her hand and the friends she hadn't seen since June.

Caroline hopped impatiently from foot to foot as she waited for the elevator. Her "school" was one flight up on the third floor in the Solarium. Her mother, Jacqueline Kennedy, wanted to protect Caroline's privacy; she wanted to keep Caroline out of the limelight and give her as normal a childhood as possible. Caroline's mother, therefore, had handpicked the students for the school, and many of them were children of old friends or children of the President's administrative staff.

Caroline and her brother John John in Hyannis Port, their first year in the White House

When the elevator opened it was already packed with Caroline's schoolmates on their way up to the classrooms.

"Caroline, Caroline! Hi, Caroline!" they all cried, and moved aside to make a small space for her. When the doors closed, Clare grabbed Caroline's hand, happy to see her after the long summer. Clare and Caroline had been best friends ever since Caroline was four years old and Clare's mother had jumped fully clothed into the swimming pool to rescue Caroline, who had paddled into the deep end and almost drowned.

"They're going to have to build a bigger elevator for us!" Clare whispered to Caroline. They both giggled.

When the door opened on the third floor, Miss Grimes, the kindergarten teacher, and Miss Boyd, the first-grade teacher, were both there waiting. While the kindergartners followed Miss Grimes down the hall to their classroom, Miss Boyd, pushing her fingers through her light brown hair, waited until a line formed. Then she turned forward and led the way to the first-grade classroom.

"Welcome back, children," she called. The noisy gaggle of twelve first graders followed their teacher to their new classroom in the Solarium.

Caroline eagerly looked for her name on the small wooden tables neatly arranged around the room. Then she ran to check the view from the floor-to-ceiling windows just to make sure the Washington Monument was still there. She carefully put away her lunch box and quietly sat down with the rest of the children. Although some of them had come from as far away as Virginia to go to school at the White House, Caroline didn't give it a second thought that her school happpened to be in the same house in which she lived. In fact, it never even occurred to her that her home just happened to be the most prestigious house in America.

The walls of the classroom were covered in light oak-wood shelving that held a colorful array of brightly colored wooden blocks, puzzles, stuffed animals, and other toys. When Miss Boyd was through showing Caroline and her classmates around the new classroom, Mrs. Smith showed up for their first activity. Caroline knew Mrs. Smith because she had taught the rhythm class last year while Caroline was in kindergarten. Caroline dashed to her cubby to find her dancing clothes: pale blue leotards just like the other girls'. The boys wore shorts and shirts. Mrs. Smith hauled out the long blue mats and laid them on the floor across the length of the room.

*President Kennedy,
Caroline, John John,
and Macaroni*

"Yeah! Somersaults!" Anthony Radziwill, one of Caroline's first cousins, shouted. Immediately Caroline joined one of the two lines that formed. One by one, she and the other children tucked themselves into tight balls and rolled head over heels, just like roly-poly bugs. Caroline's favorite part of rhythm class was the routines they did on the gray-tiled floor. Barefoot, she and her friends danced and stretched and leapt to the rhythm of their teacher's tom-tom.

After rhythm class was storytime. All the children crowded around Miss Boyd. Caroline waved her hand wildly in the hope that Miss Boyd would call on her to choose the story for the day. Caroline always picked horse stories. Like her mother, she loved horses. She had her own horse, Macaroni, who often grazed on the front lawn of the White House. She rode Macaroni as much as she could. Her mother was a proficient horsewoman and was determined that Caroline would be a good rider too. After school, on the South Lawn, Caroline's mother would teach her how to "sit" a horse and how to hold the reins. Sometimes Caroline was allowed to ride on her own without a lead line. On weekends, at their country home near Middleburg, Virginia, Caroline would ride Macaroni and follow her mother around the four hundred wooded acres.

During mid morning recess, Caroline and the others went out onto the third-floor balcony. Most of them headed straight for the tricycles, except for Caroline, who always looked for the hobby horse. In the downstairs garden playground, there was a jungle gym and a tree house. And behind a huge, blood-red rhododendron bush, which Caroline knew had been planted especially to provide them with privacy from passers-by on the street, was a trampoline which she loved to jump on.

Often Caroline and her classmates would pay a visit to her father's office, which wasn't far from the playground. Evelyn Lincoln, her father's secretary, had a sparkling smile which was a warm welcome to Caroline. Mrs. Lincoln would hold out the small glass dish full of candy that was always on her desk.

Because Caroline's school was located in the White House, there were times that she and all the children became a part of the history that was created there. One time, when Caroline and her friends were still in kindergarten, the President had arranged a red-carpet welcome ceremony on the White House lawn for President Ahmed Ben Bella of Algeria. The Marine Band was playing, and a group of specially invited guests had gathered. It was a beautiful, sunny day, and Caroline and her classmates were allowed to watch the ceremony from behind the balustrade of the Truman balcony. As the cymbals crashed and the drums rolled, Caroline became increasingly involved, and so did the others. During the traditional twenty-one gun salute, after each cannon was fired, Caroline and the children shouted, "Boom!" When her father and President Ben Bella reviewed the troops lined up in their military uniforms, Caroline and her friends, totally caught up in the ceremony, shouted, "Present arms! A-ttention!"

That same year, ten Native American delegates to the National Congress of the American Indian put on a special war dance at the White House, dressed in their colorful traditional costumes. Caroline's class sat with her mother on the floor to watch the dancers as their feathers flew, their headdresses shook, and their feet moved around the circle of children. Caroline's little brother, John John, had skipped preschool that day in order to watch the dancing.

Bob Burnett, a Rosebud Sioux and director of the National Congress, scooped up Caroline's brother in his arms and introduced him to all the other chieftains. Then Caroline and the other girls curtsied to the chieftains while the boys bowed from their waists. Some of her friends were so excited that they insisted on shaking hands with the Native Americans over and over again.

Another time when Caroline and her classmates were on their way out to play, they passed the Diplomatic Reception Room. When Caroline peered in, she saw a large group of Korean children. Some of them looked almost as young

President Kennedy, Caroline, and John John in the Oval Office

as her, while others looked much older. Her mother invited her class in and introduced them to the World Vision Korean Orphan Choir. Caroline's mother persuaded the choir to perform for the children. As Caroline's small class of friends sat on the floor, the choir sang "Rudolph, the Red-Nosed Reindeer" in phonetic English and "Korean Lullaby" in their native language. Caroline was entranced.

During any school day, when Caroline heard the roaring blades of the President's helicopter as it circled the White House to land on the South Lawn, she would race to the window and try to catch a glimpse of it.

"Your daddy's home!" one of the children would shout to Caroline as they crowded around her at the window. As President of the United States, her father traveled a lot. Caroline knew that his being home meant she might be able to stay up a little later that night in order to spend time with him.

President Kennedy's helicopter landing on White House lawn

Most days after school, Caroline ate lunch with her mother. On a lucky day, her dad would walk across from his next-door office to join them. Unless his back was bothering him, Caroline always ran up to him and was in his arms before anyone could say "Jack Robinson."

Caroline's father always liked a big lunch, a bowl of fish chowder or a broiled lamb chop, mashed potatoes, and a green vegetable. Caroline would sometimes share his lunch. She would eat everything except for the green vegetable.

Evenings in the Kennedy household were always different. On those early evenings when her parents were not at home, Caroline was allowed to watch TV. Her favorite program was *Bozo the Clown*. Occasionally while she switched the stations, Caroline caught sight of a newsreel of her father. She would shout for Nannie Shaw to come and see, and she laughed as she watched him smiling out at the crowds of people who were always nearby. Sometimes she would run over and plant a kiss on his face.

On those evenings when her father was home she would join her parents in their second floor study during their cocktail hour. Nannie Shaw would bring in John John for a few minutes after his bath, so her parents could tell him good night. Then Caroline would read to herself from one of the picture books that were stacked neatly on the lower shelves of the bookcase, while her mother and father enjoyed their cocktail hour. Sometimes, they even let Caroline have her own "cocktail," which was, of course, soda pop. Then she would rush off to bathe and change into her pajamas. She would return to the sitting room and curl up in her father's arms as he read her "Snow White" or "Goldilocks and the Three Bears." Even though she had heard them each at least a thousand times before, they were still her two favorite stories, especially when her dad was the reader.

1963–1969
LYNDON BAINES JOHNSON

Wedding Bells for Luci

*I*t was the evening before Luci Baines Johnson's big day. Gathered in the White House Solarium, comfortably dressed in shifts and slacks, were Luci; her older sister, Lynda Bird; her mother, Lady Bird; her soon-to-be mother-in-law, Mrs. Nugent; and her bridesmaids. In the same room where Luci had entertained her friends with the blaring strains of the Beatles' "She Loves You" and the soft melody of Burt Bacharach's "What the World Needs Now," there was a splendid buffet, spread out on a long table with a beautiful yellow-flowered centerpiece. Crabmeat crêpes, tomato baskets filled with chicken salad, and fresh fruit garnished with sugared grapes and mint leaves had been arranged. All the young women, along with Luci's mother and Mrs. Nugent, sat around in chairs and on the sofa to watch as Luci distributed the gifts she'd gotten for them.

Beginning with her sister and going from bridesmaid to bridesmaid, Luci handed each a small, carefully wrapped package. As each one opened her gift, she would either screech with delight or jump up to hug and kiss Luci. Luci had bought them gold bracelets with an ornate charm in the shape of a floral bouquet, set with tiny deep-pink rubies in the center. Inscribed on the back was the name of the bridesmaid and "A bouquet of friendship and love—Luci 8/6/66."

While they ate, Luci and her friends reminisced about her past three years in the White House. Beth Jenkins asked Luci if she remembered her first night there. Beth had helped Luci move into her new room, and she had been invited to spend that first night with Luci. It had been a long and tedious day of moving, and everyone except Luci and Beth had gone off to bed. After they changed into their nightgowns, Luci decided to light the fire that had been carefully laid in her bedroom fireplace. What could be nicer after a long, hard day than to sit in front of a crackling fire, talking with one of her oldest friends, she had thought. She lit the fire and stood back to watch. As the kindling caught, smoke began to pour out of the fireplace and into the room. Soon the room was so clouded with smoke that neither Luci nor Beth could see one another. Luci made her way to the bedroom door and yanked it open. She began to shout for help. All over the second floor, doors opened and slammed while the nearly hysterical Johnson family "flapped about" until J.B. West, the White House Chief Usher, appeared and put out the fire. The next day he carefully explained to Luci how to open the fireplace damper to give the smoke its proper vent.

Lynda Bird, who was taller than Luci but had the same thick raven-colored hair, remembered the good times, but she also spoke of the hardships. She reminded Luci how, for the first six months after they had moved in, the Solarium was still being used as a schoolroom for Caroline Kennedy and her friends. Luci remembered how hard it had been to live in the White House while the two Kennedy children and everyone else around them mourned the loss of Jack Kennedy. Along with the continuous talk of Kennedy's assassination, their grief had seeped through the huge house.

When their father had been Vice-President, Luci and her sister had always been under the watchful eyes of the Secret Service. But when their father became President, the Secret Service never left their side. Lynda Bird's Secret Service code name was "Gypsy" and Luci's was "Venus." When Lynda Bird went off to college the Secret Service still followed her to every class, to lunch, and on weekends, to parties. They were ever present. Luci pointed out that every word the girls spoke, everything they wore, everything they did, every single boy they even said hello to, became public knowledge. Luci no longer had any privacy. She also remembered the daily barrage of peace marchers and demonstrators—the "longhairs," hippies, college students, and "regular folks" who always seemed to be out front of the White House with their picket signs and voices, screaming things like "Hell, no! We won't go!" and "Hey, Hey, LBJ! How many kids have you killed today?" They were protesting the Vietnam War, never letting any of

Protest at the White House, 1966

the Johnsons forget for even a moment that they felt United States involvement in the war was wrong.

"Remember the time our whole history class came to tour here?" one of Luci's friends asked. Luci had gone to a private school called National Cathedral, which was not far from the White House. On one occasion she had invited all sixty-two members of her class to come see where she lived. She had shown them the second-floor kitchen and even given them a quick glimpse of her bedroom, which had amazed her mother, who was never allowed to show *anyone* Luci's room while conducting her own White House tours.

Another one of the girls reminded Luci about the surprise party that two of their friends, Stevie Steinert and Bill Hitchcock, had given her the night after she graduated from high school. Luci had had plans to go up to Camp David, the White House weekend retreat, that evening with a group of her girlfriends. She had come home with her friends from the graduation ceremony, promptly rolled her hair in curlers, and dressed in a huge sloppy shirt and shorts. While she was relaxing with her friends and sitting under a hair dryer in her room, unbeknownst to her, people had begun arriving for the party and were being sneaked upstairs to the Solarium. Stevie and Bill had collected a list of about forty of Luci's friends and invited them all to come. They had decorated the Solarium and set up cocktail tables, chairs, and candles. The party was supp-posed to start at nine o'clock sharp.

Meanwhile, Luci had decided to stay dressed exactly as she was for the drive up to Camp David, curlers and all. Her friends couldn't figure out how to get her to change her clothes and brush out her hair. And nobody could figure out

President Lyndon Johnson and Luci outside the White House

how to get her up to the Solarium. Even Luci's mother was at a loss as she frantically ran upstairs and down between Luci and her girlfriends, the State Dining Room where Luci's father was entertaining former President Eisenhower and fifty guests, and the Solarium to make certain Stevie and Bill had everything they needed for the surprise party.

Finally, somebody came up with a simple solution to the problem. Her girlfriends merely told her there was somebody waiting to see her upstairs, whereupon Luci brushed out her hair, changed her clothes, and unsuspectingly appeared for her party.

After more laughter and reminiscing, Luci and her guests retired to the theater to watch an old movie, *Home from the Hill*, starring Lynda Bird's boyfriend, George Hamilton. Luci had intended an early evening for them all, but with her bridesmaids spending the night at the White House, she found that neither she nor anyone else was ready for bed.

In the middle of the movie, they were interrupted by Luci's father, who came in with her fiancé, Pat, and Pat's father, Mr. Nugent. The President had taken Pat, his father, and all the young men who were to be in the wedding to a private room at D.C. Stadium called The Dugout. They had had their own buffet of hamburgers, hot dogs, and soft drinks while they watched the ball game.

The next morning dawned sunny and bright—a picture-perfect morning for a wedding. Luci was up early to get ready, as was everyone else. A vintage screen had been rescued from a musty White House storage room and stretched across the East Hall to conceal the women's dressing area, complete with tables, mirrors, chairs, and hair dryers. The bridesmaids wore their robes while their hair was teased into high beehive hairdos. Luci ate breakfast while her hair stylist teased her hair into a soft "bubble" style which held her veil securely in place.

One of her bridesmaids asked if she had gathered the necessary and traditional "Something old, something new, something borrowed, something blue."

Luci's treasured "something old" was being guarded by Helen, one of her best friends. Her great-grandmother Ruth Ament had made a rose-point lace handkerchief fifty-eight years ago. This was Luci's link with her grandmother's family and, as tradition demanded, she would slip it in her sleeve when she walked down the aisle.

Her long white wedding gown was her "something new," and a rosary given to Lynda by Pope John XXIII was her "something borrowed." Her "something blue" was a gold locket tied with a blue satin ribbon that belonged to Mrs. Nugent and held photos of Pat and his brother Jerry, Jr., when they were babies. On a friend's suggestion, Luci also placed an English sixpence in her shoe for good luck. As Luci sat quietly, she thought about all the raucous parties she had had in the Solarium and wondered if her days of dancing the Watusi were over.

Suddenly Lynda Bird jumped up and began fluttering her arms as she danced around the hall singing, "Get Me to the Church on Time," from the musical *My Fair Lady*. Luci rolled her eyes and everyone laughed.

Downstairs in the State Dining Room, the huge old crystal chandelier had been intertwined with clusters of delicate white flowers. In the lavishly decorated basement, Luci's wedding gifts were displayed for all of her guests to look at during the reception. Three long tables, covered with elaborate white damask tablecloths made especially for the occasion, were laden with a variety of gifts from friends, family, and Luci's admirers. Former President and Mrs. Truman had sent a silver bun warmer; Luci's uncle Tony had sent a set of sherbet cups that had belonged to his mother, Luci's grandmother; Willie Day Taylor, a family friend and press office staffer, had sent her a heavy iron skillet which was already well seasoned from many years of use; and there were crocheted pot holders and handkerchiefs edged with tatting made by schoolchildren and senior citizens who knew Luci only through the newspapers and television but wanted to let her know they cared.

One gift, not on display, had been given to Luci and her fiancé the day before. It was a government savings bond in a generous amount, and on the envelope the President had written, "To our children who bring us so much joy and strength."

On the freshly painted walls of the basement, Jim Ketchum, the White House curator, had set up a framed pictorial display of all the White House

President Johnson, Lynda, and Luci on Luci's wedding day

brides arranged chronologically. There were Maria Monroe Gouverneur, 1820; Lizzie Tyler Waller, 1842; Julia Gardiner Tyler, 1844; Nellie Grant Sartorio, 1874; Frances Folsom Cleveland, 1886; Alice Roosevelt Longworth, 1906; Jessie Wilson Sayre, 1913; and Eleanor Wilson McAdoo, 1914.

Finally, everyone was ready to go to the church, and the Mansion was ready for the festive reception to follow. In front of the White House, in the morning heat, long black limousines waited to take the family and wedding party to the church. Luci paused and smiled for a brief moment. Luci had become a member of the Catholic church, as was Pat, several years before. Their wedding was held in the National Shrine of the Immaculate Conception Church with the traditional Catholic ceremony, including the offering of Holy Communion at the close of the service. Pope Paul VI had even sent a telegram of congratulations from the Vatican in Rome, which was read at the completion of the ceremony.

After the couple made their promises to each other, they began their walk down the aisle. Pat waited as Luci stopped to kiss her mother and give her a rose from her bouquet, then Luci kissed her father. She crossed to the other side of the aisle, kissed Mrs. Nugent, and gave her a rose. As Luci and her husband made their way down the stairs and through the smiling and cheering crowd that waited to congratulate them, her attention was momentarily diverted once again by the marching protesters. She could hear their determined yells, even above the cheering good wishes of the crowd around her, and she glimpsed the reality of her life and her father's: No matter what they might be doing in their personal lives, somehow the whole world was a part of it.

Luci realized that she had mostly gotten used to it. But just for an instant she wondered what it would have been like to have had a "normal" life, a "normal" wedding, without the eyes of the world upon her.

A Secret Place for Amy

The huge sprawling limbs of an old cedar near the White House held the tree house Amy Carter and her father had designed. It wasn't a terribly complicated tree house, but it was large enough to sleep three or four girls comfortably and had all the essentials—like walls and a door. Most importantly, it was up high enough so that Amy could see both the world below and the stars and the sky above. And furthermore, it was absolutely private.

Tonight nine-year-old Amy would have her first sleep over there with Claudia Sanchez, her best friend, and Mary Fitzpatrick, Amy's long-time nursemaid. The weather had been fine for March and the forecaster predicted that it would be a mild evening. Amy tucked the first load of blankets under her arm as she climbed up the wooden slats that had been nailed on the tree for stairs. She had already brought up some popcorn and a bag of her favorite cookies.

It had only been a couple of months since Amy and her family had moved into the White House, and during that time Amy had started a new school, found a new best friend, and acquired a new dog. At first she had been both angry and sad that her father had been elected President. While he had been governor of Georgia, she had eventually gotten used to the spotlight. She had marched in parades and driven in motorcades since long before she could read or

Amy Carter poses with her family for a Christmas portrait.

write. But the truth was that she didn't like the attention. On election night, when Amy had snuggled down in her own bed in Plains, Georgia, she had prayed that her father would lose.

At 3:30 that morning, when her mother and father awakened her to tell her that her father had been elected, Amy had cried. She cried because she didn't want to leave Plains. She cried because she didn't want to leave her school or the friends who had been her friends all her life. And she cried because she didn't want to leave Grandma Lillian. Amy knew enough to appreciate what she was leaving behind. She was sure that no matter how hard everyone tried to make her life "normal," being the daughter of the President of the United States was even more unique than being the daughter of the governor of Georgia. It meant she was different, and being different was hard.

Both of her parents did their best to make the move a smooth and pleasant one for Amy. Even though her brothers were quite a bit older, married, and living on their own when their father was elected President, two of the three moved into the White House with Amy and her parents. Unlike most of the other first families, Amy's parents didn't bring any of their furniture from Plains to the White House, and her mother didn't do much redecorating.

Her parents liked the White House just the way it was, with all of its history.

Amy's room was on the second floor, almost directly across from her mother and father's room. Her older brother Chip and his wife, Caron, lived with their baby in a three-room suite on the third floor, as did Amy's brother Jeff and his wife, Annette. Amy's oldest brother, Jack, who was twenty-nine when his father was elected President, had stayed in Georgia.

Taking another pile of blankets to the tree house, Amy passed Mary Fitzpatrick in the stairwell. Mary asked her if she needed any help. When Amy shook her head, Mary put her smooth hand affectionately on Amy's shoulder and told her she was looking forward to the evening's sleep over.

"Me too!" Amy said, and smiled.

Mary had started working for Amy's parents while they lived in the Governor's Mansion in Georgia. But Mary's work had been interrupted when one weekend, while visiting a small Georgia town, she had been involved in a street fight in which a man she had never seen before was killed. Mary was convicted of murder and was sent to jail. After he became President, Amy's father had contacted the Pardon and Parole Board in Georgia to ask them to release Mary from

*Amy with
Mary Fitzpatrick*

prison and allow her to come work for them in Washington. President Carter was convinced that Mary had been serving a sentence for a crime she hadn't committed, and he felt a strong desire to help her. Amy liked Mary and admired her father's courage in bringing a "criminal," as some people saw Mary, to the White House. She was glad Mary had come to live with them.

Amy's tree house was not visible from the street, and the overgrown foliage on the cedar branches kept Amy mostly hidden from the White House staff as well. She liked this privacy and intended only to share it with her closest friends. As she climbed up the wooden slats of the tree with the last load of blankets under her arm, she wondered if she should bring her dog, Grits, and her cat, Misty Malarky Ving Vang, for the sleep over.

A few months before, Amy had received a letter from her soon-to-be teacher, Verona Meeder. Amy had still been in Plains, and Mrs. Meeder had written to tell her about her new school. She had also told Amy that her dog had given

Amy in her tree house with her nephew and her father.

birth to nine puppies, and she was offering them to anyone in the class who might want one. The first born of the litter had come just after it was announced on TV that Amy's father had been elected President. Mrs. Meeder had named the puppy Grits, and she wanted to know if Amy would like to have him.

Amy felt lonely that first day of school in Washington. The sky had been dark, and her jeans had rubbed against her raincoat as she dragged her Snoopy book bag up the school stairs. There had been a mass of TV cameras and news reporters who had come to film her as she entered her new school. Amy had kept her head down, and, afterward, the reporters had agreed with her mother that it was best to leave Amy alone. Everyone had seen how uncomfortable she was. She had been ten minutes late because of rush-hour traffic, and her mother had apologized profusely to Mrs. Meeder, saying it would never happen again. All the children in the class were silent as they stared at Amy, the new girl, the daughter of the President.

But after only a few moments in the room Amy said, "Hey, ya'll, when can I get Grits?"

That very afternoon, Mrs. Meeder, her husband, and their teenage son and daughter had taken the puppy to the White House.

Amy met Claudia Sanchez her first morning at school. Mrs. Meeder had arranged the children so that Claudia sat right next to Amy. Apparently Mrs. Meeder thought Amy would appreciate Claudia's quiet manner and maturity. And she was right. The two girls liked each other immediately. From that day forward, Amy, with her long, shiny blond hair, and Claudia, with her huge brown eyes and brown hair, were fast friends. At school they ate lunch together every day, and they were partners on every field trip. Amy spent as much time with Claudia as she could.

Claudia was the daughter of one of the cooks at the Chilean Embassy. Amy didn't go to Claudia's house often, due to security problems, but Claudia spent a lot of time with Amy at the White House. Amy loved it.

The first time Amy brought Claudia home from school, they had gone down to the screening room and watched *Freaky Friday,* a Disney film. Afterward they had gone bowling in the basement bowling alley.

Amy told Claudia the stories she had heard about the White House ghost. Some said it was Lincoln's ghost, and that it stalked the second floor. Once when Claudia had spent the night, the two girls had brought a Ouija board into the Lincoln Room, and, after trying to conjure up his spirit, decided to sleep in the

Amy roller-skating on
White House driveway

huge Lincoln bed. Not being ready to sleep in the room by themselves, they had convinced Mary Fitzpatrick to join them. About midnight they were all absolutely positive they had heard footsteps, but, frozen with fear in the bed, none of them dared get up to see.

The next morning, Amy showed Claudia the "secret stairway" and how to push the special panel in the wall which opened the door to the stairs. But after their adventure the night before, neither of them had the nerve to follow where the stairs led.

It was almost 6:00 P.M., and Claudia was expected for the outdoor sleep over any minute. Amy was excited. She thought she had time for one last trip to the tree house with a stack of new books. Amy loved to read, and her dad had recently given her *The Phantom Tollbooth* and *The Twenty-one Balloons*. She knew that she and Claudia probably wouldn't get around to reading because they spent most of their time together talking and laughing. Amy would save the books to read when she was alone in the tree house.

Through the tree's branches Amy could glimpse both the Washington Monument and the Lincoln Memorial. She knew the story about Jesse Grant, and how his father, President Ulysses S. Grant, had given Jesse a small shed at the bottom of the garden where he and his friends had held their secret meetings. She had also heard how Quentin Roosevelt and his White House Gang had roamed the same area when Quentin's dad, Theodore Roosevelt, had been President.

While Amy was admiring her view, her mother called out to say that her friend had arrived. Her mother and father were on the Truman Balcony, where they often sat in the late afternoons. Amy knew her parents had the same view as she did, and, according to Amy's father, it was "the best view in the house."

Amy inched her way down the wooden slats. Soon she was racing through the wide halls of the White House to the front door.

"Claudia, I'm coming!" Amy called.

Amy, Claudia, and Mary had a wonderful time in the tree house that night, the first of many to come. And Amy found that she finally had her own private place, untouchable by the press and hidden even from most of the White House staff. When Amy was in her tree house, most of the time she felt just like any other kid.

Glimpses of Chelsea

It was May 1994, and although the bitterness of the winter months in Washington had passed, it was still cool. The dogwoods were coming into bloom, and the sky was clear and blue. At Sidwell Friends School the children were out on the blacktop playground, building wooden-framed booths for the annual carnival. The sound of hammers and the hum of voices surrounded Chelsea Clinton as she dipped her paintbrush again and again into a can of black paint and slowly and precisely printed "Fortunes" on a wooden board. She and another girl had volunteered to be the carnival gypsies, to read palms and tell fortunes next Saturday afternoon. Chelsea and her friends yelled cheerfully across the playground to one another as they helped ready the school for the carnival.

It had been over a year since Chelsea and her parents moved from their home in the Governor's Mansion in Little Rock, Arkansas, to Washington, D.C. During the first few weeks, Chelsea had walked the wide White House hallways and wondered if she could ever call it home. It had felt more like a museum with all the historic furniture everywhere. She missed her grandparents, who had stayed in Little Rock. Soon after her father had become President and they moved from Arkansas, Chelsea's grandfather had suffered a stroke and died.

Chelsea's Cat, Socks

Chelsea and her mother had flown back to Arkansas for the funeral. Her father had needed to stay in Washington in order to run the country. It was a very sad time for Chelsea.

Although Chelsea had made many friends at her new school, those first few months had been especially lonely and hard. Even though being the daughter of the President allowed her many privileges, which included being able to have her Little Rock friends visit her in the White House, she had longed to be able to go back and forth to their houses as easily as when she had lived there. Now with the Secret Service trailing her most of the time, she definitely missed her privacy.

Even before Chelsea left Little Rock, she and her parents had begun discussing schools for her in Washington. Initially, they all felt it would be fine for her to go to a public school. After all, her parents were firm believers in public education and felt she should set an example by attending a public school as she had in Little Rock. But after careful consideration, they all agreed that with the Secret Service ever present, Chelsea was bound to stand out and draw a lot of attention. It was decided that a private school would be more comfortable. And at Sidwell Friends, there were children of other public officials, including those of senators and representatives. Chelsea wouldn't be quite so different.

One of Chelsea's new friends told her later that before she arrived at Sidwell, all the teachers and kids had been preparing for her. The kids were asked not to talk about her behind her back and not to discuss her with the reporters who had already begun to hang around. Some of her friends even admitted that in the beginning they had felt their freedom was being taken away, for when Chelsea first arrived, all the classroom doors had to be locked from the inside and opened and locked again if someone came in late. Everyone had to knock and give their names at the door. Some of Chelsea's friends said they had felt put out, so they made up passwords like "swordfish" or used expressions like "Have the lambs stopped crying?" from the movie *The Silence of the Lambs* to rebel against the restrictive arrangements of security.

The school organized "sensitivity training," and the kids met in small groups. The teachers said, "Pretend you're Chelsea," and asked each of them questions such as, "Would you want to try out for the school play? Would you want to be friends with someone like you?" Many of the kids had become concerned that she was going to be difficult to be around and that she might even be *really* weird. No one knew what to expect. None of them had ever "hung out" with a President's daughter.

Chelsea arrives with her parents.

But soon after Chelsea arrived, one of her friends told the press, "The locked-door rule was lifted, and day-to-day life hasn't changed at all. Once she got on campus, we realized she was just a kid like the rest of us. The Secret Service watches her outside, not in class. She's friendly, nice to everybody, she can be real funny, and she's bright for her age."

As Chelsea and her friends put lids back on the paints and tidied up, a bell rang interrupting the carnival preparations, and immediately the playground became a blur of jeans, T-shirts, and Doc Martens scuffling across the blacktop. It was lunchtime, and the children were all eager for food and a break.

Making her way along the hallways with her friends in tow felt easy and comfortable to Chelsea. They talked about the upcoming

Chelsea at Sidwell Friends School with her classmates

carnival and the softball game. Her new friends were fast becoming old friends. She'd gone through one soccer season with them, one baseball season, and of course the ever-continuing ballet lessons after school. Last Christmas she and some of her friends had even been in the National Ballet Company's production of *The Nutcracker*.

Chelsea had gotten used to calling 1600 Pennsylvania Avenue home. She and her parents had made some changes in the White House that helped to make it feel more like their own. They'd turned the pantry on the second floor, where President Truman's family had stored some of their food, into a small breakfast room. Now they didn't have to eat all their meals in the enormous Dining Room. Chelsea had asked the White House painters to paint her room blue and white. And she and her mother had decided that if the huge crystal chandelier that hung from the high ceiling were replaced by smaller brass lamps, the room would feel more like a teenager's room. Of course, Chelsea put her TV and cassette and CD players where she could blast the sounds of 10,000 Maniacs and Boyz II Men as loud as she wanted—within reason that is.

On her thirteenth birthday, she'd had a sleep over with several friends who flew in from Little Rock, as well as new friends from Sidwell Friends. They spent the night laughing and talking about all kinds of silly things. That party and others helped make some of the harder moments of being the President's daughter seem easier.

When Chelsea had first come to Washington, she and her parents had talked about how difficult it could be to deal with the press. Although Chelsea knew her parents would do everything in their power to protect her, there were bound to be difficult times with the media, particularly if they didn't like the way either of her parents was handling some political matter. Then the press would probably pick on her.

Sure enough, one reporter made a big deal of the fact that, the day before the inauguration when the First Family was at church, Chelsea had fallen asleep and snored. And after the inauguration, when Chelsea had gone to the MTV Ball and everyone started yelling, "Chel-sea! Chel-sea!" this same reporter had commented that he was surprised at how utterly embarrassed she was. Other stories came out in newspapers and magazines about her hair and her braces, and Chelsea discovered some of the hurtful aspects of being in the limelight and being the daughter of the President.

The White House mail room received hundreds of letters for Chelsea each day from children all over the United States who wrote to tell her how worried they were about her life in the White House:

Dear Chelsea,

Hi! My name is Katie! I know just how you feel. My dad was the mayor of the town where I live, Blasdell. I always got bugged by someone no matter where I went! Isn't it annoying? It drove me crazy! People were always saying, "Oh! Are you the

Chelsea in the Washington Ballet's performance of The Nutcracker. *She played the Favorite Aunt.*

mayor's daughter?" I didn't want my dad to be the mayor anymore. I mean, I was
happy for him, but I didn't like it. Is that the way you feel?

Well, I'm sure it will all work out for you.

> *Yours truly,*
> *Katie McGuire*
> *Blasdell, New York*

They were worried about the Secret Service following her around and her loss of privacy:

Dear Chelsea,

My name is Alana Wilson. I go to Lake Dolloff Elementary, in Washington State.
I'm in the fifth grade, and overjoyed about writing to Chelsea. I've been the daughter
of someone very important many, many times, and sometimes it's not very fun. My
mom is a manager at Boeing in Seattle, and on the weekends when I go to work with
her, if she's not with me she sends an employee from the third floor to watch over
me–kinda like a bodyguard. But I just grin and bear it, thinking to myself, "It'll be over
soon," and try not to complain. 'Cause I want to stay irresponsible until they start pil-
ing the jobs on me!!

> *Sincerely,*
> *Alana Wilson*
> *Auburn, Washington*

And they were worried about how mean the press was being to her:

Dear Chelsea,

I heard about people making fun of you. I know how you feel. People used to make
fun of me because I was big and tall. Just ignore them! I found out people were calling
me names just for a laugh. They laughed because I would get upset and sometimes cry.
The next day when they called me a name I didn't get upset. They stopped calling me
names because they didn't get their laughs anymore.

> *Sincerely,*
> *David Noles*
> *Lynchburg, Tennessee*

P.S. Don't worry about your braces. I've got braces too. I also wanted to tell you
you're very pretty.

Of course, some of them just wanted to know what it was like to be the

President's daughter—what her favorite foods were and what it was like to meet all those famous people who came to the White House each day. They wanted to know what a normal day was like for her.

Sometimes Chelsea was tempted to answer some of the letters and tell these kids that she loved broccoli, macaroni and cheese, baked potatoes, fried chicken, chocolate cake, and Mexican food. She would have said that she loved math and science and wanted to be an astronaut when she grew up. She wanted to tell them that she got home from school around 3:00 P.M., and after her snack she started her homework. She would have written that, aside from doing her homework in the small room next to the Oval Office called the Presidential Study and being able to use the White House Library, which had 2,600 mostly leatherbound books, during the school week her life was very much the same as any of her friends.

But Chelsea quickly recognized that her life was also quite different than her friends. Just like her parents, Chelsea realized that she was now an example to kids around the nation in the way she looked and acted. When her teachers and the student body talked about setting up a recycling center in school, Chelsea and her family had already done that. All the offices in the White House now had recycling bins for newspaper, plastic, aluminum, and glass, as well as corrugated paper envelopes and computer paper. Her parents' long term environmental plans included installing solar panels so that the sun would heat the White House tap water. The White House staff had been slowly changing all the light bulbs so they would be extra "energy efficient."

Being in the limelight sometimes has given Chelsea an advantage while at other times it has made her wish her life was more "normal."

Carnival day came around fast and with it a fairly warm and sunny Saturday. The playground was a mass of color, and the wooden booths were now covered with festive tents that flapped in the breeze. Chelsea was dressed up in a white lace blouse with short, tight, puffy sleeves; a brightly colored skirt fell in soft folds to below her knees. She sat in her booth at a table with a crystal ball the size of a tennis ball. It stood on a small black pedestal waiting to be used. In the booth next to her, one of her friends was the other gypsy. A long line soon formed in front of Chelsea, but her friend had no one waiting to see her.

As Chelsea read each person's palm or looked deeply into their eyes, she told

The Clintons go white-water rafting

them things like, "You have strange hands," "You won't live long," "Your heart will start to fail when you're sixty," or "Your love life won't start until you're forty." To one boy she said, "You will marry at forty-five and have a couple of kids." She was having fun with her "gypsy power."

Pretty soon Chelsea noticed there was still no line in front of her friend's gypsy booth. She wondered how she might feel if no one stood waiting to have their fortunes told by her. She knew she would be crushed. So she quickly excused herself from her booth and her own long line and left for awhile, hoping that the kids would line up in front of her friend's booth while she was gone.

Sometimes it's hard to be the President's daughter, Chelsea thought as she walked around looking at the other booths. There were moments when she wasn't sure if her friends liked her because she was Chelsea or because she was Chelsea Clinton, First Child and daughter of the President of the United States of America. There were times when she longed to be back at home in Little Rock, in a simpler life, curled up on her bed with her fuzzy, black-and-white cat, Socks, just like any other teenager.

When Chelsea returned, she noticed that a line had formed in front of her friend's booth, and she smiled. As she sat down in her own booth and resumed her role as a fortune-teller, she thought about her own future; like any other fourteen-year-old's, so much of hers was unknown. Would she dance in *The*

Nutcracker again? What position would she play on the soccer team next season? Would her father be reelected, and would they return to Little Rock if he wasn't?

One thing Chelsea did know was, at least for now, she would have to deal with both the comforts and discomforts of being a First Child and of living in the White House with the eyes of the world and the press on her most of the time. She was getting used to it and probably even beginning to like it. After all, she was the daughter of the President of the United States. There was an honor in that. Summer wasn't too far off. There were elaborate plans being made for summer camp in Colorado. And, like any other teenager, that was something Chelsea was looking forward to.

Afterword

GEORGE WASHINGTON

Just before her grandfather's eight-year term as President ended, Nellie decided she preferred to be called Eleanor to sound more sophisticated. She married Lawerence Lewis, George Washington's favorite nephew, and lived at Woodlawn, an estate not far from Mt. Vernon that her grandfather had given her. Eleanor continued to play the harpsichord.

George Washington Parke "Little Wash" Custis was twenty-three years old when he married. He built a home on the west side of the Potomac River and lived the life of a country gentleman. His home was called Arlington, which is today surrounded by the nation's most important military burial ground, the Arlington National Cemetery. He and his wife had a daughter who married Robert E. Lee.

THOMAS JEFFERSON

After giving birth to her second child, Thomas Jefferson's younger daughter, Maria Eppes, died at age twenty-five in 1804 at Monticello. Her father was still in office.

Jefferson's elder daughter, Martha, married a man she had known all her life, Thomas Mann Randolph, and gave her father many grandchildren. After his Presidency, Thomas Jefferson continued to love and cherish his remaining daughter and grandchildren. He gave his granddaughters Ellen and Cornelia silk dresses, and Virginia, a guitar. Martha's oldest son, Thomas Jefferson "Jeff" Randolph, eventually moved to a farm only two miles from his grandfather's home in Monticello. To ensure frequent visits, the former President had a smooth road paved between the two properties.

When Thomas Jefferson died in 1826, his daughter Martha inherited his estate, which was heavily in debt. Her husband, who had been governor of Virginia, died two years later, leaving her a destitute widow. Martha threatened to sell Monticello to pay the debts, but she was saved by cash gifts totaling over $20,000 from the states of Louisiana and South Carolina. And her son Jeff, a devoted grandson, vowed to pay off all of his grandfather's debts. Jeff also looked after his younger brothers and saw that they were properly educated, while his mother taught his sisters.

Anne married Charles Lewis Bankhead. She died in 1829, a few months before her grandfather, and in 1836 Martha died of a stroke.

Ellen grew up to marry Thomas Coolidge, and her sister Virginia married Nicholas Trist. Both of their husbands became well-known diplomats and wealthy men.

Virginia, although married and settled in Washington, made it a point to spend a portion of each year in Boston with her sister Ellen.

Thanks to Martha "Patsy" Randolph, eleven of whose children lived to adulthood, Thomas Jefferson has more descendants living today than any other President.

John Tyler

Mary Tyler, John Tyler's oldest daughter, died young at thirty-three in 1848.

Robert moved to Philadelphia, practiced law, and formed a voluntary military regiment to fight in the 1846 Mexican War. When the Civil War broke out, he fled from Philadelphia and was threatened with hanging. Robert became Register of Treasury for the Confederate states, editor of the Montgomery *Advertiser,* and finally head of the Democratic party in Alabama. While they lived in the White House, he and his wife, Priscilla, had one daughter, Mary Fairlee. He died in 1877 at the age of sixty-one.

John, Jr., became Assistant Secretary of War, but spent much of his life trying to surpass his older brother's accomplishments. He died in 1896 at seventy-six.

Letitia divorced her husband, James Semple, a Confederate spy and womanizer, ran a school for girls in Baltimore called The Eclectic Institute, and lived longer than any of her other siblings, dying at the age of eighty-five in 1907.

Elizabeth, known as "Lizzie," married William Waller in a White House wedding. After her mother's death, like her sisiter Letitia, she would not at first acknowledge her father's marriage to Julia Gardiner. Unlike the rest of the Tylers, in time Lizzie came to be quite friendly with her father's second wife. In 1850 she died from complications arising from childbirth. She left five young children.

Although many considered the heavy Alice less than glamorous, after her father left office she became a flirt, finally marrying a clergyman and giving birth to one daughter before she died at twenty-seven in 1854.

Tazewell became a surgeon and traveled throughout the South and California, dying in 1874 from alcoholism. He was forty-three years old.

John Tyler had five sons and two daughters by his second wife, Julia, all of whom lived to adulthood.

Abraham Lincoln

Unlike Abraham Lincoln, who worked for everything he achieved, Robert made his fortune because of his father's name. After his father's assassination, Robert practiced law in Illinois, became a business executive with the famous Pullman Palace Car Company, and worked closely as a political aide and Cabinet member for various Republican Presidents, including James Garfield and Chester Arthur.

After his father was shot, Tad seemed to change overnight from an irresponsible youngster into a serious-minded youth. He studied hard and became his mother's greatest comfort. They lived in Chicago and went to Germany for a year, where Tad studied with a tutor and had a chance to make up for his lack of formal education. Tad lost all traces of his lisp by eighteen. Shortly after his return to the United States, he developed diptheria or pneumonia (sources do not agree) and died on July 15, 1871.

ANDREW JOHNSON

Martha Johnson Patterson, assisted by her widowed sister, Mary Johnson Stover, did a lot for the prestige of the White House. The two women gave the nation's first house the glamour we now associate with the President's home. They devoted a good deal of time to decorating and modernizing the interior of the White House.

After Johnson's presidency, Martha and her family lived in the Johnsons' Greeneville, Tennessee, home. Martha died in 1901 at seventy-two. Mary visited and comforted many veterans in the aftermath of the Civil War. She remarried and settled in Bluff City, Tennessee, to oversee a family cotton mill.

Charles, the eldest Johnson son, a pharmacist and medic, had taken his own life during the Civil War in 1863, two years before his father became President. He was thirty-three years old.

At the end of his Presidency, Andrew Johnson moved back to Tennessee with his two daughters. Mary Johnson Stover Brown and her new husband lived near enough to her parents that she could look after them for the rest of their lives.

Robert, although a very good Presidential secretary, suffered throughout his life from heavy drinking and died of alcoholism one month after his father left office. He was thirty-five years old.

Andrew "Frank" Johnson, Jr. finished his education and began a career in journalism. At only twenty-one, he published the Greeneville *Intelligencer,* but his efforts failed to produce a lucrative newspaper. Frank married, but died in 1879 at the age of twenty-six, only four years after his father. He had no children.

ULYSSES S. GRANT

Of the Grant boys, Frederick's career was the most impressive. He was appointed by President Benjamin Harrison as Minister to the Austro-Hungarian Empire and spent four years in Vienna. He also worked as Police Commissioner of New York City, fought as a colonel in the Spanish-American War, and by 1912 occupied the nation's second highest military position. He married and had two children, but died of throat cancer, as had his father, shortly before his sixty-second birthday in 1912.

After Grant's second term as President, Buck (Ulysses, Jr.), who graduated from Harvard, and Jesse, who had attended Cornell, accompanied their parents as they traveled around the world. When they returned, the Grants were involved in a financial scandal that nearly resulted in the family's bankruptcy.

Buck settled in San Diego, California, where he worked in business and participated in Republican politics. He had five children by his first wife, who died in 1913. He died in 1929 at the age of seventy-seven.

Nellie, tired of her English husband's drinking, divorced him, left Europe, and returned to the United States, where she married her girlhood sweetheart. She wrote several books about her experiences. She died in 1922 at the age of sixty-seven.

Jesse moved to Mexico, where he colonized land near Tijuana and built a casino. He also completed a book, *In the Days of My Father: General Grant*. He died in 1934 at the age of seventy-six.

RUTHERFORD B. HAYES

Birch graduated from Harvard Law School, began practicing law in New York, and finally settled in Toledo, Ohio, where he practiced tax law until his death at seventy-two in 1926. He married and had five children.

Webb turned from politics to business and became rich by building up the giant Union Carbide Corporation. Eager to live up to his father's legacy and with a thirst for war, Webb entered and was honored for his participation in the Spanish-American War, the Boxer Rebellion in China, and World War I. Before his death at seventy-eight in 1934, he established a library and museum in Fremont, Ohio, to honor his father. He married late in life and had no children.

Rutherford continued his schooling for many years and never gave up his love of libraries. He designed the first reading room entirely for children. He died in 1927 at sixty-nine years old.

After her mother's death in 1889, Fanny assumed the role of hostess and travel companion for her father and married only after Hayes's death in 1893. She had one child. She was eighty-two years old when she died in 1950.

Scott achieved success in the railroad business, and, although the youngest of the Hayes children, he was said to have had the closest relationship with his father. He died at fifty-two in 1923.

JAMES A. GARFIELD

Hal, the oldest Garfield child to survive infancy, was involved primarily with academics and became president of Williams College. He also headed the Fuel Administration for Woodrow Wilson during the First World War and later was awarded the Distinguished Service Medal. He died at seventy-nine in 1942.

James had a great love of the law. He served in the Ohio Senate and had close working relationships with Presidents William McKinley, Theodore Roosevelt, and Herbert Hoover. He married and had four children. He was eighty-four years old when he died in 1950.

Following her heart, Mollie married her father's secretary, Stanley Brown, settling in New York City, and later, Pasadena, California. She was eighty years old when she died in 1947.

After graduating from Williams, Irwin continued on to law school and later went to Boston to begin a practice. He married, had three children, and lived until he was eighty. He died in 1951.

Abram, after graduating from Williams, began postgraduate studies at Massachusetts Institute of Technology, graduating in 1896. He toured Europe to study the architecture and later established his own architectural firm. He achieved national recognition and was appointed by President Theodore Roosevelt to the National Council of Fine Arts in 1909. President Coolidge named Abram to the National Fine Arts Commission in 1925. He remarried at the age of seventy-five. He died in 1958 at the age of eighty-five.

THEODORE ROOSEVELT

The wife of a congressman and daughter of a President, Alice Roosevelt became an important figure in Washington society. Throughout her life she was both loved and hated for her outlandish personality. She had one child and lived the longest of any of the First Children to date. She died at the age of ninety-six in 1980.

Fulfilling his father's wishes, Ted was trained as a military officer and honored in World War I. He was involved in politics, serving as Assistant Secretary of the Navy and Governor of Puerto Rico. Ted later rejoined the army as a Brigadier General to aid the Allies during World War II. He died in 1944 at fifty-six.

After his father's Presidency, Kermit traveled with his father on big game hunts in Africa. He escaped politics, but fought in both the First and Second World Wars. He also worked in the steamship business. He died at fifty-three in 1943.

Ethel married a doctor and worked for the American Ambulance Corps in Paris during World War I. In later years she supported the Republican Presidential nomination of Richard Nixon. She had four children. She died at eighty-six in 1977.

Like his two older brothers, Archie fought in both world wars and was an avid Republican supporter and businessman. He married and had four children. He died in 1981 at the age of eighty-seven.

Although many of the Roosevelt children lived long into their eighties and nineties, Quentin, a combat pilot, was shot down over France during World War I, dying at the age of twenty in 1918.

WILLIAM HOWARD TAFT

The eldest Taft, Robert, attended both Harvard and Yale universities, but, although he served as Senate Majority Leader, he never achieved his dream of reaching the White House. Robert opposed Franklin Roosevelt's New Deal and helped pass the Taft-Hartley bill in 1947, which placed restrictions on organized labor. He married and had four children. He was sixty-three years old when he died in 1953.

Helen Herron Taft Manning was an outstanding woman. After attending Bryn Mawr College, Helen acted as the White House hostess. She married Dr. Frederick J. Manning, earned a master's degree from Yale, and became the dean of Bryn Mawr. Both an academic and a domestic, Helen personified the new American woman at a time when women gained both respect and full citizenship by winning the right to vote. She had two children.

Charlie studied law at Yale, fought for the army during World War I, and later became mayor of Cincinnati. While he disagreed with his brother Robert on many issues, he was loved and respected by his own community. He married and had seven children.

Lillian Rogers Parks grew up and worked as a maid at the White House. She wrote a book about her experiences titled *My Thirty Years Backstairs at the White House*, and lives in retirement in Washington.

CALVIN COOLIDGE

After graduating from Amherst College, where he boxed, acted, and sang, John worked for the New York, New Haven, Hartford Railroad. He later headed a small manufacturing company. John also carried out his mother's plans to give the Coolidge home in Plymouth, Vermont, to the state of Vermont so it could be opened to the public. In 1995 John was eighty-eight and still living in Vermont. He recently celebrated his sixty-fifth wedding anniversary

Cal's life ended sadly at sixteen while his father was out on the road, campaigning for reelection. Soon after blistering his toe while playing tennis in sneakers without socks on the White House grounds, Cal acquired blood poisoning and never recovered. The Coolidges mourned deeply for the loss of their son.

FRANKLIN DELANO ROOSEVELT

Anna remarried twice. With her second husband, a journalist, she struggled to run a small newspaper, the *Arizona Times*, which eventually failed. Her third husband was a professor and a physician. Her only children, Sistie and Buzzie, were from her first husband. She died in 1975 at the age of sixty-nine.

James worked in business and insurance and, while his father was still in the White House, as president of Goldwyn Studios. He later settled in Southern California, where he became involved in politics. He married three times, and had three children by his first wife. He died in 1991.

After only four years of military service, Elliott was honored with the status of Brigadier General. He was later accused of failing to pay off a $200,000 debt; wrote a book entitled *As He Saw It* about his father; and became mayor of Miami Beach during the 1960s. He was married four times, with one child by his first wife and three by his second. He died the year before his brother James.

Franklin, Jr., campaigned for John F. Kennedy and acted as Assistant Secretary of Commerce. He led a life devoted to social causes, heading the Equal Opportunities Commission under President Johnson and serving as a member of the U.S. Civil Rights Commission. He was also a congressman for New York. He was married four times, with two children by each of his first two wives. He died in 1988.

John worked in business as an executive for the clothing chain Filene's Sons and later gave his support to the Republican party. He was married twice, with three children by his first wife. He died in 1981 at the age of sixty-five.

Sistie became a librarian and teacher at a school for the handicapped. She married Van H. Seagraves of Oregon, and they lived in Paris for several years. She had three children and was living in Lake Placid, New York, in 1995.

Buzzie, who chose to use the name "Roosevelt" rather than "Dall," worked in New York for the American Association for the United Nations. He was living in New York City in 1995.

Diana Hopkins, who for five years enjoyed all the privileges of a grandchild in the Roosevelt household, attended Bryn Mawr College. She also studied in Switzerland and at the School of Foreign Service at Georgetown University.

DWIGHT DAVID EISENHOWER

After a career in the military, John devoted his life to literary pursuits. He worked for Doubleday Publishing, and then began writing, mostly about his father. Today he appears in television commercials promoting insurance for veterans.

John's son David attended Phillips Exeter Academy and graduated with honors in 1966. He went to Amherst College rather than West Point as his father and grandfather had. He married Julie Nixon, the daughter of President Richard M. Nixon, in a White House wedding, and has two children.

After the White House years, John's three daughters took part in equestrian activities, winning many horse shows, and they remain close as a family.

JOHN FITZGERALD KENNEDY

After President Kennedy's death, Caroline's mother married a wealthy Greek businessman, and the family traveled throughout the world. Caroline attended Radcliffe College and is now a lawyer, married, and the mother of three. She is also the author of two books and the president of the John Fitzgerald Kennedy Library Foundation.

John John, as an energetic young boy, mimicked the Beatles and loved to play cowboys and Indians. He later attended Brown University and Harvard Law School, and went to work for the District Attorney's office of New York. Then he decided to try his luck at acting and hosted a documentary on the plight of the homeless in America. He has just launched a political magazine named *George*. Like his sister, he is actively involved in the John Fitzgerald Kennnedy Library Foundation. Both he and his sister serve on a committee that selects the recipient of the "Profiles in Courage" Award.

Three months before his assassination, John Kennedy and his wife, Jackie, had a son they named Patrick Bouvier. Patrick lived only two days.

Both the Kennedy children were at their mother's bedside when Jacqueline Kennedy Onassis died in May 1994.

LYNDON BAINES JOHNSON

The older of Johnson's daughters, Lynda, did not immediately accept her father's success as a politician. She had an eating disorder and tried several times to reinvent her public self. But following her sorority days at the University of Texas and her military wedding to a Marine Corps officer, Lynda worked for *McCall's* magazine and then became chairwoman of the Presidential Advisory Committee for Women under President Carter. Lynda's husband, Charles Robb, was elected governor of Virginia in 1982 and senator in 1988.

A tough-minded young woman, Luci married a Vietnam veteran, Patrick Nugent. The marriage lasted thirteen years, and they had four children. Luci is remarried and now lives in Austin, Texas, not far from her widowed mother.

JAMES EARL "JIMMY" CARTER

John practices law in Calhoun, Georgia, and runs a grain storage business. He has always been active in his father's political career and may, in the future, enter into America's political arena.

James Earl "Chip" III, after having been an avid supporter of his father during the Presidency, today feels his upbringing suits him well for a life in politics. He plans to enter the race for the Georgia legislature in the near future.

Jeff has never really been in the public eye. After graduating from college, he founded a computer consulting firm. He has since achieved considerable success.

After being badly treated by the national press as a youngster and causing political problems for her father while in the White House, Amy Carter attended Brown University, where she spent most of her time on radical political activities. She left before graduating. Amy now lives in Plains, Georgia.

WILLIAM JEFFERSON "BILL" CLINTON

Chelsea, the only child of President and Hillary Rodham Clinton, lives in the White House and attends the Sidwell Friends School in Washington, D.C., as of this writting. She loves soccer and dancing, and, in the winter of 1993, appeared on the cover of *The New York Times* performing in a Washington rendition of *The Nutcracker.*

The Presidents' Children

Most of our Presidents had children. Some of those children were grown and had children of their own during their father's terms, others weren't born until years after, and a few were adopted. The list that follows is meant to complete the picture I began with the stories in this book. Presidential grandchildren have been named below only when they have been included in those stories.

TERM OF OFFICE: 1789–1797

George Washington m. Martha Dandridge Custis

President and Mrs. Washington, who had no children of their own, raised two children of Martha's deceased son John Custis.

      Eleanor "Nellie" Custis . . . 1779–1852

      George Washington Parke "Little Wash" Custis . . . 1781–1857

TERM OF OFFICE: 1797–1801

John Adams m. Abigail Smith

      (Abigail) Amelia "Nabby" "Emmy" . . . 1765–1813

      John Quincy . . . 1767–1848

      Susanna . . . 1758–1770

      Charles . . . 1770–1800

      Thomas Boylston . . . 1772–1832

TERM OF OFFICE: 1801–1809

Thomas Jefferson m. Martha Wayles Skelton

      Martha Washington "Patsy" . . . 1772–1836 (m. Thomas Mann Randolph)

            Anne Carey . . . 1791–1826

            Thomas Jefferson "Jeff" . . . 1792–1878

            Ellen . . . 1796–1876

            Cornelia . . .1799–1871

            Virginia . . . 1801–1882

            Mary . . . 1803–1876

            James Madison . . . 1806–1834

            Benjamin Franklin . . . 1808–1871

            Meriwether . . . 1810–1837

            Septima Anne . . . 1814–1887

            George Wythe . . . 1818–1867

      Jane Randolph . . . 1774–1775

      Mary "Maria" "Polly" . . . 1778–1804 (m. John Wayles Eppes)

            Frances . . . 1801–1881

Lucy Elizabeth I . . . 1780–1781

Lucy Elizabeth II . . . 1782–1785

Thomas and Martha Jefferson also had an unnamed son who died within weeks of his birth in 1777.

TERM OF OFFICE: 1809–1817

James Madison m. Dorothea "Dolley" Payne Todd

They had no children.

TERM OF OFFICE: 1817–1825

James Monroe m. Elizabeth Kortright

Eliza Kortright . . . 1786–1835

J.S. . . . 1799–1801

Maria Hester . . . 1803–1850

TERM OF OFFICE: 1825–1829

John Quincy Adams m. Louisa Catherine Johnson

George Washington . . . 1801–1829

John II . . . 1803–1834

Charles Francis . . . 1807–1886

Louisa Catherine . . . 1811–1812

TERM OF OFFICE: 1829–1837

Andrew Jackson m. Rachel Donelson Robards

Andrew "Andy," Jr. (adopted) . . . about 1808/09–1865

TERM OF OFFICE: 1837–1841

Martin Van Buren m. Hannah Hoes

Abraham . . . 1807–1873

John . . . 1810–1866

Martin "Mat," Jr. . . . 1812–1855

Smith Thompson . . . 1817–1876

TERM OF OFFICE: 1841 *(Died after one month in office)*

William Henry Harrison m. Anna Tuthill Symmes

Elizabeth Bassett . . . 1796–1846

John Cleves Symmes . . . 1798–1830

Lucy Singleton . . . 1800–1826

William Henry, Jr. . . . 1802–1838

John Scott . . . 1804–1878

Benjamin . . . 1806–1840

Mary Symmes . . . 1809–1842

Carter Bassett . . . 1811–1839

Anne Tuthill . . . 1813–1845

James Findlay . . . 1814–1817

TERM OF OFFICE: 1841–1845

John Tyler m. Letitia Christian

Mary . . . 1815–1848

Robert . . . 1816–1877

John, Jr. . . . 1819–1896

Letitia . . . 1821–1907

Elizabeth "Lizzie" . . . 1823–1850

Anne Contesse . . . 1825–1825

Alice . . . 1827–1854

Tazewell "Taz" . . . 1830–1874

m. Julia Gardiner

David Gardiner "Gardie" . . . 1846–1927

John Alexander "Alex" . . . 1848–1883

Julia Gardiner . . . 1849–1871

Lachlan . . . 1851–1902

Lyon Gardiner . . . 1853–1935

Robert Fitzwalter "Fitz" . . . 1856–1927

Pearl "Pearlie" . . . 1860–1947

TERM OF OFFICE: 1845–1849

James K. Polk m. Sarah Childress

They had no children

TERM OF OFFICE: 1849–1850 *(Died in office)*

Zachary Taylor m. Margaret Mackall "Peggy" Smith

Anne Margaret Mackal. . . . 1811–1875

(Sarah) Knox . . . 1814–1835

Octavia Pannel . . . 1816–1820

Margaret Smith . . . 1819–1820

Mary Elizabeth "Betty" . . . 1824–1909

Richard "Dick" . . . 1826–1879

TERM OF OFFICE: 1850–1853

Millard Fillmore m. Abigail Powers

(Millard) Power. . . . 1828–1889

Mary Abigail "Abby" . . . 1832–1854

m. Caroline Carmichael McIntosh

TERM OF OFFICE: 1853–1857
Franklin Pierce m. Jane Means Appleton

      Franklin . . . February 2–5, 1836

      Frank Robert . . . 1839–1843

      Benjamin "Benny" . . . 1841–1853

TERM OF OFFICE: 1857–1861
James Buchanan

He was our only bachelor president.

TERM OF OFFICE: 1861–1865 *(Assassinated)*
Abraham Lincoln m. Mary Todd

      Robert Todd "Bob" . . . 1843–1926

      Edward Baker . . . 1846–1850

      William Wallace "Willie" . . . 1850–1862

      Thomas "Tad" . . . 1853–1871

TERM OF OFFICE: 1865–1869
Andrew Johnson m. Eliza McCardle

      Martha . . . 1828–1901

      Charles . . . 1830–1863

      Mary . . . 1832–1883

      Robert . . . 1834–1869

      Andrew "Frank," Jr. . . . 1852–1879

TERM OF OFFICE: 1869–1877
Ulysses S. Grant m. Julia Boggs Dent

      Frederick Dent . . . 1850–1912

      Ulysses Simpson "Buck" Jr. . . . 1852–1929

      Ellen Wrenshall "Nellie" . . . 1855–1922

      Jesse Root . . . 1858–1934

TERM OF OFFICE: 1877–1881
Rutherford B. Hayes m. Lucy Ware Webb

      (Sardis) Birchard Austin "Birch" . . . 1853–1926

      (James) Webb Cook . . . 1856–1934

      Rutherford Platt "Rud" . . . 1858–1927

      Joseph Thompson . . . 1861–1863

      George Crook . . . 1864–1866

      Frances "Fanny" . . . 1867–1950

      Scott Russell . . . 1871–1923

      Manning Force . . . 1873–1874

TERM OF OFFICE: 1881 *(Assassinated)*
James A. Garfield m. Lucretia "Crete" Rudolph
       Eliza Arabella "Trot" . . . 1860–1863
       Harry Augustus "Hal" . . . 1863–1942
       James Rudolph "Jim" . . . 1865–1950
       Mary "Mollie" . . . 1867–1947
       Irwin McDowell . . . 1870–1951
       Abram . . . 1872–1958
       Edward "Neddie" . . . 1874–1876

TERM OF OFFICE: 1881–1885
Chester A. Arthur m. Ellen Lewis "Nell" Herndon
       William Lewis . . . 1860–1863
       (Chester) Alan II . . . 1864–1937
       Ellen Herndon "Nell" . . . 1871–1915

TERM OF OFFICE: 1885–1889 and 1893–1897
Grover Cleveland m. Frances Folsom
       Ruth "Baby Ruth" . . . 1891–1904
       Esther . . . 1893–1980
       Marion . . . 1895–1977
       Richard Folsom "Dick" . . . 1897–1974
       Francis Grover . . . 1903–

TERM OF OFFICE: 1889–1893
Benjamin Harrison m. Caroline Lavinia Scott
       Russell Benjamin . . . 1854–1936
       Mary Scott "Mamie" . . . 1858–1930
             m. Mary Scott Lord Dimmick
       Elizabeth . . . 1897–1955

TERM OF OFFICE: 1897–1901 *(Assassinated)*
William McKinley m. Ida Saxton
       Katherine "Katie" . . . 1871–1875
       Ida . . . April 1–August 22, 1873

TERM OF OFFICE: 1901–1909
Theodore Roosevelt m. Alice Hathaway Lee
       Alice Lee . . . 1884–1980
             m. Edith Kermit Carow
       Theodore "Ted," Jr. . . . 1887–1944

Kermit . . . 1889–1943

Ethel Carow . . . 1891–1977

Archibald Bulloch "Archie" . . . 1894–1979

Quentin . . . 1897–1918

TERM OF OFFICE: 1909–1913

William Howard Taft m. Helen "Nellie" Herron

Robert Alphonso "Bob" . . . 1889–1953

Helen Herron . . . 1891–1987

Charles Phelps "Charlie" . . . 1897–1983

TERM OF OFFICE: 1913–1921

Woodrow Wilson m. Ellen Louise Axson

Margaret Woodrow . . . 1886–1944

Jessie Woodrow . . . 1887–1933

Eleanor Randolph . . . 1889–1967

m. Edith Bolling Galt

TERM OF OFFICE: 1921–1923 (*Died in office*)

Warren G. Harding m. Florence Mabel "Flossie" Kling DeWolfe

They had no children.

TERM OF OFFICE: 1923–1929

Calvin Coolidge m. Grace Anna Goodhue

John "Butch" . . . 1906–

Calvin "Cal," Jr. . . . 1908–1924

TERM OF OFFICE: 1929–1933

Herbert Hoover m. Lou Henry

Herbert Clark, Jr. . . . 1903–1969

Allan Henry . . . 1907–1993

TERM OF OFFICE: 1933–1945 (*Died in office early during his fourth term*)

Franklin Delano Roosevelt m. (Anna) Eleanor Roosevelt

Anna Eleanor . . . 1906–1975 (m. Curtis Dall)

Anna Eleanor "Sistie" . . . 1927–

Curtis "Buzzie" . . . 1930–

James "Jimmy" . . . 1907–1991

Franklin . . . March 18–November 8, 1909

Elliott . . . 1910–1990

Franklin Delano "Brud," Jr. . . . 1914–1988

John Aspinwall . . . 1916–1981

TERM OF OFFICE: 1945–1953

Harry S Truman m. Elizabeth Virginia "Bess" Wallace

(Mary) Margaret "Margie" . . . 1924–

TERM OF OFFICE: 1953–1961

Dwight David Eisenhower m. Mary Geneva "Mamie" Doud

Dwight Doud . . . 1917–1921

John Sheldon Doud . . . 1923– (m. Joanne Thompson)

Dwight David II . . . 1948–

Barbara Anne . . . 1949–

Susan Elaine . . . 1951–

Mary Jean . . . 1955–

TERM OF OFFICE: 1961–1963 *(Assassinated)*

John Fitzgerald Kennedy m. Jacqueline Lee Bouvier

Caroline Bouvier . . . 1957–

John Fitzgerald "John John," Jr. . . . 1960–

Patrick Bouvier . . . August 7–9, 1963

TERM OF OFFICE: 1963–1969

Lyndon Baines Johnson m. Claudia Alta "Lady Bird" Taylor

Lynda Bird . . . 1944–

Lucy Baines "Luci" . . . 1947–

TERM OF OFFICE: 1969–1974 *(Resigned from office early in second term)*

Richard M. Nixon m. Thelma Catherine "Pat" Ryan

Patricia "Tricia" . . . 1946–

Julie . . . 1948–

TERM OF OFFICE: 1974–1977

Gerald R. Ford m. Elizabeth Anne "Betty" Bloomer

Michael Gerald "Mike" . . . 1950–

John Gardner "Jack" . . . 1952–

Steven Meigs . . . 1956–

Susan Elizabeth . . . 1957–

TERM OF OFFICE: 1977–1981

James Earl "Jimmy" Carter m. (Eleanor) Rosalyn Smith

      John William "Jack" . . . 1947–

      James Earl "Chip" III . . . 1950–

      Donnell Jeffrey "Jeff" . . . 1952–

      Amy Lynn . . . 1967–

TERM OF OFFICE: 1981–1989

Ronald W. Reagan m. (Sarah) Jane Wyman (divorced 1948)

      Maureen Elizabeth . . . 1941–

      Michael Edward (adopted) . . . 1945–

          m. Nancy Davis (b. Anne Francis Robbins)

      Patricia Ann "Patty" . . . 1952–

      Ronald Prescott . . . 1958–

TERM OF OFFICE: 1989–1993

George Herbert Walker Bush m. Barbara Pierce

      George Walker, Jr. . . . 1946–

      Pauline Robinson "Robin" . . . 1949–1953

      John Ellis "Jeb" . . . 1953–

      Neil Mallon . . . 1955–

      Marvin Pierce . . . 1956–

      Dorothy Koch "Doro" . . . 1959–

TERM OF OFFICE: 1993–

William Jefferson "Bill" Clinton m. Hillary Rodham

      Chelsea . . . 1980–

Selected Bibliography

General Overview

Aikmen, Lonelle. *The Living White House.* 7th edition. Washington: White House Historical Association, 1982.

Cavanah, Frances. *They Lived in the White House.* Philadelphia: Macrae Smith, 1961.

Colman, Edna. *Seventy-five Years of White House Gossip, From Washington to Lincoln.* New York: Doubleday, Page, 1925.

Cross, Wilbur and Ann Novolny. *White House Weddings.* New York: McKay, 1967.

Devitt, George Raymond, comp. *The White House Gallery of Official Portraits of the Presidents, McKinley Memorial Edition.* New York: Gravure Company of America, 1901.

Donovan, Hedley. *Roosevelt to Reagan.* New York: Harper & Row, 1985.

Fisher, Leonard Everett. *The White House.* New York: Holiday, 1989.

Furman, Bess, *White House Profile.* Indianapolis: Bobbs Merrill, 1951.

Garrison, Webb. *A Treasury of White House Tales.* Nashville: Rutledge Hill Press, 1986.

Hoover, Irvin Hood. *Forty-two Years in the White House.* Boston: Houghton Mifflin, 1934.

Hurd, Charles. *The White House: A Biography.* New York: Harper & Brothers, 1940.

Jenson, Amy LaFollette. *The White House and Its Thirty-four Families.* New York: McGraw Hill, 1970.

Jones, Robert. *The Presidents' Own White House Cookbook.* Chicago: Culinary Arts Institute, 1973.

Kelly, C. Brian. *Best Little Stories from the White House.* Vermont: Montpelier, 1992.

McConnell, Jane and Burt. *Our First Ladies.* New York: Crowell, 1961.

Means, Marianne. *The Women in the White House.* New York: Random House, 1963.

Parks, Lillian Rogers. *My Thirty Years Backstairs at the White House.* New York: Fleet, 1961.

Sadler, Christine. *Children in the White House.* New York: Putnam, 1967.

Seale, William. *The President's House: Volume I & II.* Washington, D.C.: The White House Historical Association & National Geographic Society, 1986.

Smith, Margaret Bayard. *The First Forty Years of Washington Society.* New York: Frederick Ungar, 1965.

Sullivan, George. *How the White House Really Works.* New York: Scholastic, 1990.

West, J.B. *Upstairs at the White House.* New York: Warner, 1973.

Willets, Gilson. *Inside History of the White House.* New York: Christian Herald Bible House, 1908.

Washington

Bourne, Miriam Anne. *Nelly Custis's Diary.* New York, Coward, McCann & Geoghegan, 1974.

Decatur, Stephen, Jr. *Private Affairs of George Washington. From the Records and Accounts of Tobias Lear, Esquire, His Seer.* Boston: Houghton Mifflin, 1933.

Flexner, James Thomas. *George Washington: Anguish & Farewell (1793–1799).* New York: Little, Brown, 1969.

Freeman, Douglas Southall. *Washington—An Abridgement in One Volume by Richard Harwell of the Seven Volume George Washington.* New York: Scribner, 1968.

Laughlin, Florence. *Skyrockets for the President.* Chicago: Rand McNally, 1973.

Lossing, J. Benson. *Memoirs of Washington by His Adopted Son, George Washington Custis.* New York: Derby and Jackson, 1860.

Moore, Charles. *The Family Life of George Washington.* New York: Houghton Mifflin, 1926.

Jefferson

Boykin, Edward, ed. *To The Girls & Boys: Being the Delightful, Little Known Letters of Thomas Jefferson To and From His Children and Grandchildren.* New York: Funk & Wagnalls, 1964.

Brodie, Fawn. *Thomas Jefferson.* New York: Norton, 1974.

Glubok, Shirley. *Home & Child Life in Colonial America.* New York: Macmillan, 1969.

Graf, Henry. *Thomas Jefferson.* New York: Silver Burdett, 1968.

Weymouth, Lally, ed. *Thomas Jefferson: The Man, His World, His Influence.* London: Weidenfeld & Nicholson, 1973.

Tyler

The Letters and Times of the Tylers. Vol. 1, 2, 3. Richmond: Whitlet & Shepperson, 1884, 1896.

Waldrup, Carole Chandler. *The Presidents' Wives.* New York: McFarland, 1989.

Lincoln

Brooks, Noah. *Washington in Lincoln's Time.* New York: Century, 1895.

Freedman, Russell. *Lincoln: A Photobiography.* New York: Clarion, 1987.

Keckley, Elizabeth Hobbs. *Behind the Scenes.* (Reprint of 1868 ed.) New York: Arno, 1968.

Kimmel, Stanley. *Mr. Lincoln's Washington.* New York: Bramfall House, 1957.

Mereditt, Roy. *Matthew Brady's Portrait of an Era.* New York: Norton, 1982.

Monjo, F. N. *Me, and Willie & Pa: The Story of Abe Lincoln.* New York: Simon & Schuster, 1973.

Turner, Justin G. and Linda Lovitt Turner. *Mary Todd Lincoln: Her Life and Letters.* New York: Knopf, 1972.

Weaver, John. *Tad Lincoln, Mischief Maker in the White House.* New York: Dodd, Mead, 1963.

Andrew Johnson

Dewitt, David M. *The Impeachment and Trial of Andrew Johnson.* (Reprint of 1903 ed.) Madison: State Historical Society of Wisconsin, 1967.

Lamask, Milton. *Andrew Johnson: President on Trial.* New York: Farrar, Straus & Cudahy, 1960.

Royall, Margaret Shaw. *Andrew Johnson: Presidential Scapegoat.* New York: Exposition Press. 1958.

Stryker, Lloyd Paul. *Andrew Johnson: A Study in Courage.* New York: Macmillan, 1929.

Grant

Grant, Jesse R. *In the Days of My Father, General Grant.* New York: Harper & Brothers, 1925.

McFeely, William S. *Grant: A Biography.* New York: Norton, 1974.

Simon, John Y., ed. *The Personal Memoirs of Julia Dent Grant.* New York: Putnam, 1975.

Tory, E. B., ed. *Personal Memoirs of U.S. Grant.* New York: World, 1952.

Hayes

Eckenrode, H.J. *Rutherford B. Hayes: Statesman of Reunion.* New York: Dodd, Mead, 1930.

Geer, Emily Apt. *First Lady: The Life of Lucy Webb Hayes.* Ohio: Kent State University Press, 1984.

Garfield

Feis, Ruth Stanley-Brown. *Mollie Garfield in the White House,* Chicago: Rand McNally, 1963.

Theodore Roosevelt

Bishop, Joseph Bucklin, ed. *Theodore Roosevelt's Letters to His Children.* New York: Scribner, 1919.

Graff, Steward. *Theodore Roosevelt's Boys.* Champaign, Illinois: Gerrard, 1967.

Hagedorn, Hermann. *The Roosevelt Family of Sagamore Hill.* New York, Macmillan, 1954.

Longworth, Alice Roosevelt. *Crowded Hours: Reminiscences.* New York: Scribner, 1933.

Looker, Earle. *The White House Gang.* New York: Fleming H. Revell, 1929.

Perkins, Frances. *The Roosevelt I Knew.* New York: Viking, 1946.

Roosevelt, Edith Kermit. *Portrait of a First Lady.* New York: Coward, McCann & Geoghegan, 1980.

Taft

Parks, Lillian Rogers. *My Thirty Years Backstairs at the White House.*

Coolidge

Coolidge, Mrs. Calvin. "Home Again." *American Magazine,* vol. 109. January 1930, pp. 18-19.

———. "How I Spent My Days in the White House." *American Magazine,* vol. 108. October 1929, pp.16-17.

———. "Making Ourselves at Home in the White House." *American Magazine,* vol. 108. November 1929, pp. 20–21.

Franklin Delano Roosevelt

Adamic, Louis. *Dinner at the White House.* New York: Harper & Brothers, 1946.

Bishop, Jim. *FDR's Last Year.* New York: Morrow, 1974.

Freedman, Russell. *Eleanor Roosevelt: A Life of Discovery.* New York: Clarion, 1993.

———. *Franklin Delano Roosevelt.* New York: Clarion, 1990.

Geddes, Donald Porter, ed. *Franklin Delano Roosevelt: A Memorial.* New York: Dial Press, 1945.

Hukok, Lorena A. *The Story of Franklin D. Roosevelt.* New York: Grosset & Dunlap, 1956.

Miller, Nathan. *The Roosevelt Chronicles.* New York: Doubleday, 1979.

Roosevelt, James and Sidney Shalett. *Affectionately, F.D.R.* New York: Harcourt, Brace, 1959.

Sherwood, Robert E. *Roosevelt and Hopkins: An Intimate History.* New York: Harper, 1948.

Sullivan, William. *Franklin Delano Roosevelt.* New York: American Heritage, 1970.

Tully, Grace. *F.D.R. My Post.* New York: Scribner, 1949.

Wharton, Don, ed. *The Roosevelts.* New York: Knopf, 1934.

Eisenhower

Eisenhower, Dwight D. *At Ease: Stories I Tell to Friends.* Garden City, New York: Doubleday, 1967.

"Eisenhower's First Hundred Days." *The New York Times Magazine,* April 26, 1953, pp. 10–11.

"Eisenhower's White House." *Fortune,* vol. 48. July 1953, pp. 74–77.

Ferrell, Robert. *The Eisenhower Diaries.* New York: Norton, 1981.

Kittler, Glen D. "Follow Ike Around for a Day." *Better Homes & Gardens,* vol. 33. October 1955, p. 33.

Larson, Arthur. *Eisenhower: The President Nobody Knew.* New York: Scribner, 1968.

Smith, Merriman. *Meet Mr. Eisenhower.* New York: Harper & Brothers, 1954.

"They Promised the Children." *Newsweek,* vol. 43. April 1954, pp. 28–29.

Tully, A. F. "Ike and Mamie at Home." *Colliers,* June 20, 1953, pp. 115, 117.

"Young Eisenhowers." *Good Housekeeping,* vol. 139. October 1954, pp. 60–63.

Kennedy

Adler, Bill. *John F. Kennedy and the Young People of America.* New York: McKay, 1965.

———. *Kids' Letters to President Kennedy.* New York: Morrow, 1961.

Bishop, Jim. *A Day in the Life of President Kennedy.* New York: Random House, 1964.

Brown, Thomas. *JFK, History of an Image.* Bloomington: Indiana University Press, 1988.

"Education of Caroline." *U.S. News and World Report,* vol. 53. July 9, 1962, pp. 59–61.

"A Glimpse at Life in Today's White House." *U.S. News and World Report,* vol. 50. April 3, 1961, pp. 61–66.

Kennedy, J. L. "When Home Is the White House." *U.S. News and World Report,* vol. 50. April 24, 1961, p. 26.

"A Look Inside the White House School." *U.S. News and World Report,* vol. 55. October 7, 1963, pp. 70–72.

Martin, Ralph G. *A Hero For Our Time: An Intimate Story of the Kennedy Years.* New York: Macmillan, 1983.

Miller, Llewellyn. "Caroline Kennedy." *Redbook,* vol. 117. June 1961, pp. 34–37.

Montgomery, Ruth. "Jackie Kennedy Tells 'How I'm Raising My Children in the White House.'" *Good Housekeeping,* vol. 152. June 1961, pp. 54–57.

Schlesinger, Arthur Meier. *A Thousand Days: John F. Kennedy in the White House.* Boston: Houghton Mifflin, 1965.

Shaw, Mark. "A Week in the Life of J.F.K.'s Wife." *Life,* November 1961, pp. 32–40.

Thomas, Helen. "Caroline Kennedy's Wonderful Little White House School." *Good Housekeeping,* vol. 157. October 1963, pp. 84–85.

Lyndon B. Johnson

"In the Spotlight, Too: The Johnson Daughters." *U.S. News and World Report,* vol. 56. May 11, 1964, p. 20.

Johnson, Lady Bird. *A White House Diary.* New York: Holt, Rinehart & Winston, 1970.

Johnson, Luci. "Forced to Grow Up." *Seventeen,* vol. 25. May 1966, pp. 166–171.

Johnson, Lynda Bird. "My Life in the White House." *Look,* vol. 29. May 18, 1965, p. 98.

Mesta, Perle. "A New Life for the Johnson Girls." *McCall's,* vol. 91. May 1964, p. 24.

"Now It's Teenage Time at the White House." *U.S. News and World Report,* vol. 56. February 3, 1964, p. 14.

Sherrill, Robert. *The Accidental President.* New York: Grossman, 1967.

Young, Joanne B. "The LBJ White House." *American Home,* vol 67. March 1964, pp. 5–6.

Carter

Carter, Jimmy. *Keeping Faith: Memoirs of a President.* New York: Bantam, 1982.

Dullea, Georgia. "Tree Houses Just for Fun." *The New York Times,* April 14, 1977, p. C8.

Glad, Betty. *Jimmy Carter, In Search of the Great White House.* New York: Norton, 1980.

"A Home Style Christmas at the White House." *U.S. News and World Report,* vol. 85. December 25, 1978, pp. 72–73.

Johnson, Lynda Bird. "Amy." *Ladies Home Journal,* vol. 109. February 1992, p. 82

Jordan, Hamilton. Crisis. *The Last Year of the Carter Presidency.* New York: Putnam, 1982.

Meeder, Verona. "Amy Carter." *McCall's,* vol. 104. June 1977, pp. 126–127.

"Subdued Christmas at the White House." *U.S. News and World Report,* vol. 87. December 24, 1979, pp. 56–57.

Clinton

Allen, Charles F. and Jonathon Portis. *The Life and Career of Bill Clinton, The Comeback Kid.* New York: Birch Lane, 1992.

Bently, D.F. *Clinton: Portrait of a Victory.* New York: Warner, 1993.

Brock, David. "Living with the Clintons." *American Spectator,* vol. 27. January 1994, pp. 38–39.

Goldberg, Judy. *Dear Chelsea: Letters From Kids and What It's Like to Live in the White House.* New York: Scholastic, 1994.

Groop, Louis Oliver. "A Visit to the White House." *House Beautiful,* vol. 136. March 1994, p. 108.

Herbert, Wray. "Parent's Choice; President's Dilemma." *U.S. News and World Report,* vol. 114. January 18, 1993, p. 53.

Kantrowitz, Barbara, with Wingert Wolfberg. "The Right Choice for Chelsea." *Newsweek,* vol. 121. January 18, 1993, p. 53.

Lelyveld, Nita. "Ex-aides to Amy Carter Offer Tips to Chelsea Clinton." *Los Angeles Times.* December 27, 1992, p. A9.

Meyers, Sara. "Don't Cry for Chelsea, Washington's Blessing." *Los Angeles Times,* Campus Correspondence. December 6, 1992, p. M3.

Murphy, A. P. "An Exclusive Interview with Chelsea's Parents." *Parents,* vol. 69. May 1994, p. 22.

Rich, Frank. "Public Stages." *The New York Times,* February 28, 1993.

Shapiro, Samantha. "A Vote for the First Kid." *The New York Times,* November 9, 1992, p. A17.

Smith, Lynn. "Stepping into the Fish Bowl." *Los Angeles Times.* December 2, 1992, p. E1.

"The Turning Point." *People,* vol. 8. March 1, 1993, p. 32.

Credits

The photographs and engravings in this book are used with the permission of the following:

AP/Wide World Photos: pages 111, 126, 127, 128, 132

Calvin Coolidge Memorial Foundation, Inc.: pages 78, 79

Chicago Historical Society: page 26

Culver Pictures, Inc.: page 73

Dwight D. Eisenhower Library: pages 94, 96, 97

Franklin D. Roosevelt Library: page 86

The Historical Society of Pennsylvania: page 4

The Historical Society of Washington, D.C.: page 28

Jimmy Carter Library: pages 118, 119, 120, 122

The John F. Kennedy Library: pages 102, 103, 105, 106

Library of Congress: pages 12, 36, 40, 42, 80

Life magazine: page 98 (photograph by Hank Walker)

The Lincoln Museum: page 29

Lyndon B. Johnson Library: pages 112, 114 (photographs by Yoichi R. Okamoto)

Massachusetts Historical Society: page 10

Monticello/Thomas Jefferson Memorial Foundation, Inc.: page 16

National Archives: page 2

National Park Service, Andrew Johnson National Historical Site: page 35

National Park Service, William Howard Taft National Historical Site: page 70, 71, 72

National Portrait Gallery, Smithsonian Institution: page 5

The New-York Historical Society: page 27

The New York Public Library: pages 15, 37, 56, 57

Ohio Historical Society: page 41

Rutherford B. Hayes Presidential Center: pages 48, 49, 50, 58

Stock Montage: page 91

Theodore Roosevelt Collection, Harvard College Library: pages 62, 63, 64, 66

UPI/Bettman: pages 87, 88, 89, 95

Virginia State Library and Archives: pages 20, 22

The Western Reserve Historical Society: page 43, 54

White House Historical Association: page ix